A GRAPHIC VOCABULARY FOR ARCHITECTURAL PRESENTATION

EDWARD T. WHITE
UNIVERSITY OF ARIZONA

COLLEGE OF ARCHITECTURE
TUCSON , ARIZONA

CONTENTS

In my own architectural drawing experience I have often felt the need for a broader awareness of forms and texture indications to use in graphically simulating·my designs. Under the pressure of time, I continually find myself using the same trees, people, furniture and textures in all my drawings. This seems to be true of practitioners in general and particularly of architectural students. Motor skills and knowledge of principles for constructing the drawings are often applied to a very limited vocabulary of textures and entourage forms which are ancillary to but nevertheless important parts of architectural drawings. The situation is akin to a writer who knows his grammatical principles and can type but is aware of only a few words with which to express his message. There are ample "graphic words" in the architectural drawing language for representing building designs. These needn't be invented anew each time a presentation is needed. Many students recognize this fact by assembling graphic vocabularies from sewing pattern catalogs, newspapers, magazines and drawing books used for other purposes.

The intent of this book is to recognize this need and to endorse the concept that designers needn't be consummate artists but simply able to make decisions and choices among known principles, forms and textures to clothe their ideas in the hypothetical realism so important to communication and evaluation of architectural design.

The degree of finish of the drawing is of course dependent upon the stage of the design process where it occurs and the purpose of the drawing. Although the forms and indications here are drawn in ink and are often rendered, they may be adapted to sketches of any degree of detail, finish or medium. The vocabulary may be expanded further by reversing the orientation of the forms and reducing or enlarging their size. The user may trace the forms directly into his drawing or use them as catalysts in generating his own. Issues such as changing clothing and automobile fashion may be handled by either adapting the forms to the new trends as they evolve or stylizing the forms to exclude any reference to fashion.

The drawing section presents example assemblies of more finished (and time consuming) presentation drawings. This should not be construed as a proposal that this is the best way to present buildings. It does, however, represent an attitude about learning to draw. It is frequently argued that it is more important for students to develop a good sketch technique than to know how to render. Sketching is an integral part of the design process whereas rendering presents results. I could't agree more. I do contend however that a very effective way to learn to sketch is to learn to render first. Successful sketching is much more difficult than rendering. A good sketch technique is a further development of a rendering technique and not vice versa. One must know what could have been drawn before deciding how to suggest it or leave it out completely. A good sketch technique comes from the need to abbreviate a rendering technique due to time limitations. The confidence, discipline and control acquired in learning to render are even more important in making a good sketch. Rendering is also much easier to learn and teach than sketching because it can be presented not as an artistic endeavor where innate talent is critical to success but as a matter of logic in the choice and assembly of views, values, textures and forms.

VOCABULARY

The vocabulary chapter is the largest in the book and represents its principal purpose. The chapter is composed of the major components used to graphically communicate an architectural design. These include textures, human figures, furniture, accessories, automobiles and trees. The number of figures is meant to maximize the possibility that the user will find the textures and forms appropriate for his drawing.

TEXTURES

The wall textures are presented in elevation at large scale, in perspective and then in elevation at small scale. Each figure illustrates the material indication in sun, shade and shadow. Paving textures include materials in plan at a large scale, in perspective and in plan at a smaller scale. White spheres are used to cast shadows on the textures at the various scales. Ground textures are treated in a similar manner. Roofing is indicated in elevation, perspective and top view. White rectangular solids are used to cast shadows on the materials in the different views.

HUMAN FIGURES

Both standing and seated figures at different scales are presented. The figures may be assembled into groups of varied sizes and activities.

FURNITURE

This section contains drawings of furniture from some of the major furniture manufacturers. They are identified on the figure list. The furniture forms are divided into single seating, multiple seating, tables and tables and chairs at different scales and orientations.

ACCESSORIES

Accessories included are lighting, pottery and potted plants.

AUTOMOBILES

Views from the rear, sides and front are drawn at varied sizes and degrees of detail.

TREES

Plan indications are shown at different scales and in varied contexts. Trees in elevation are combined with trees as background.

WALL TEXTURES

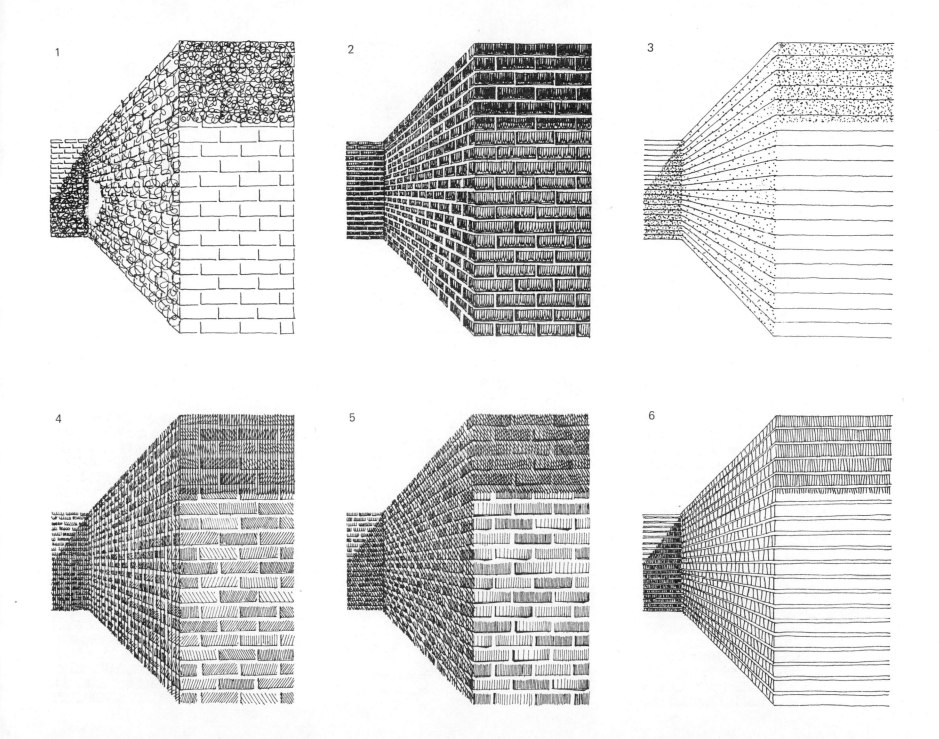

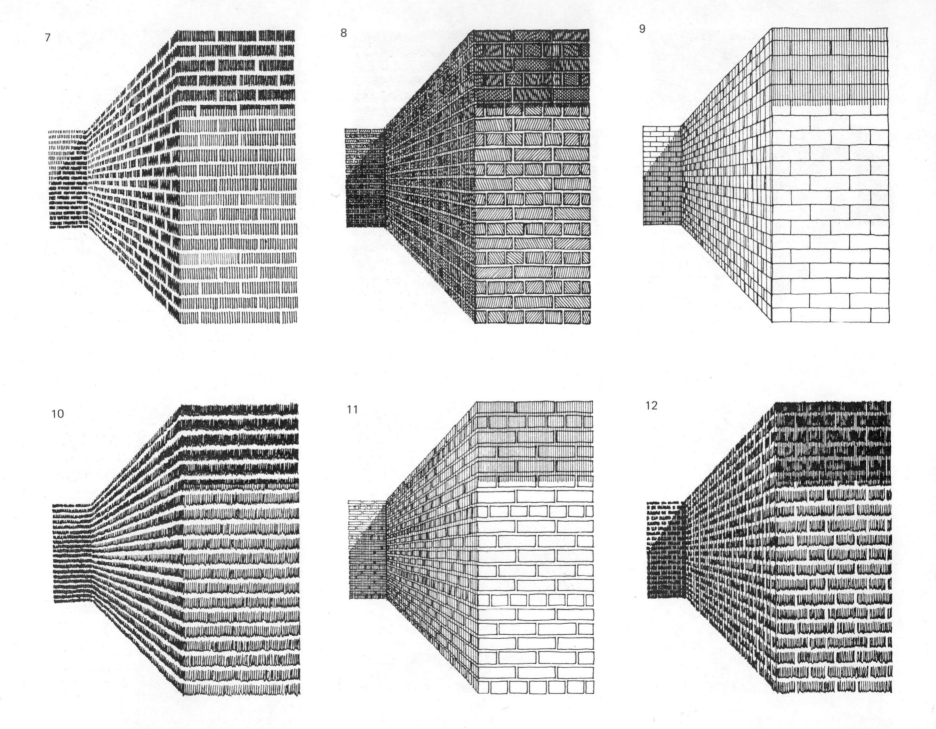

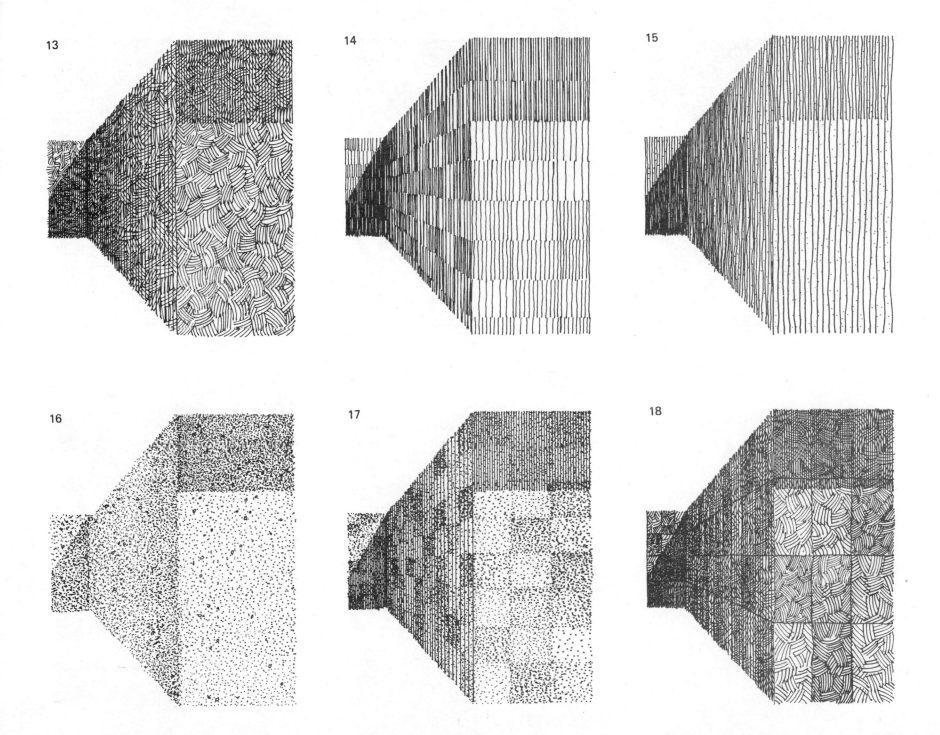

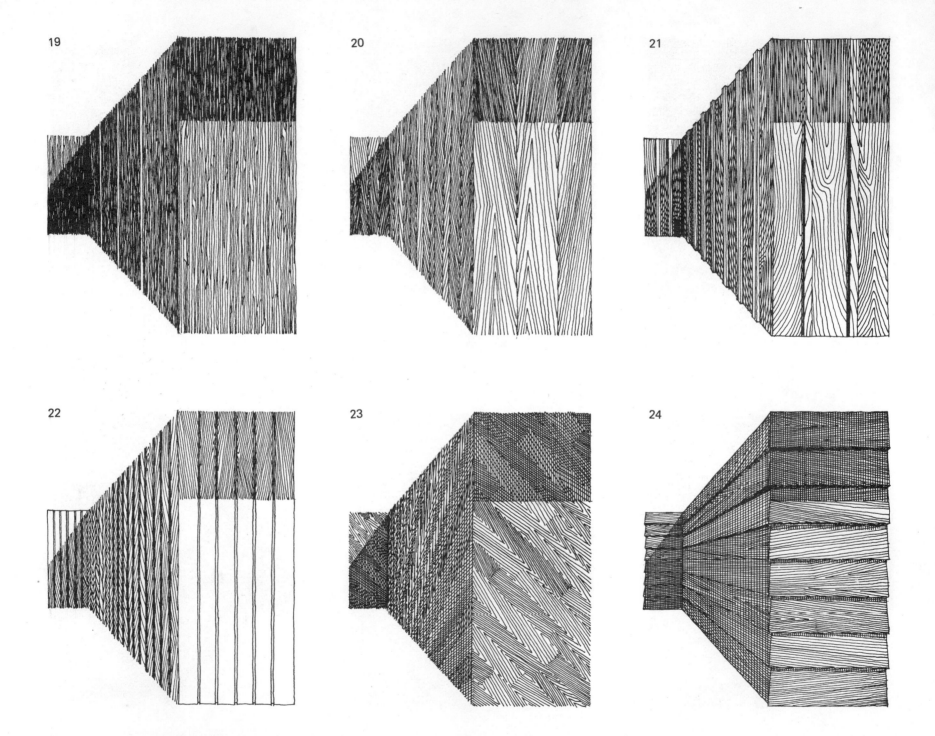

25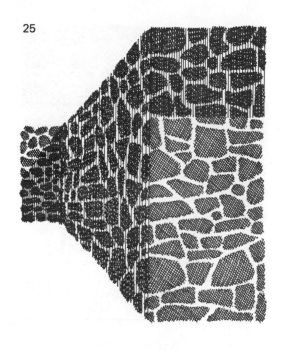

26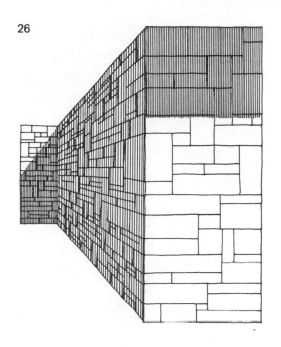

27

28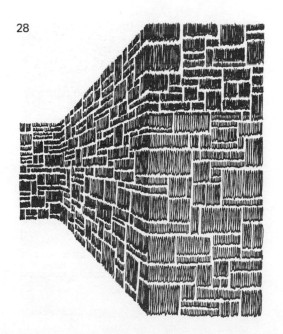

29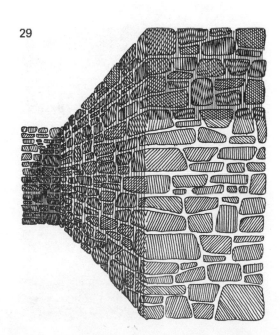

30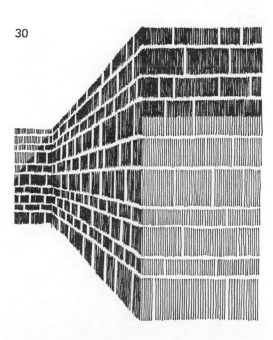

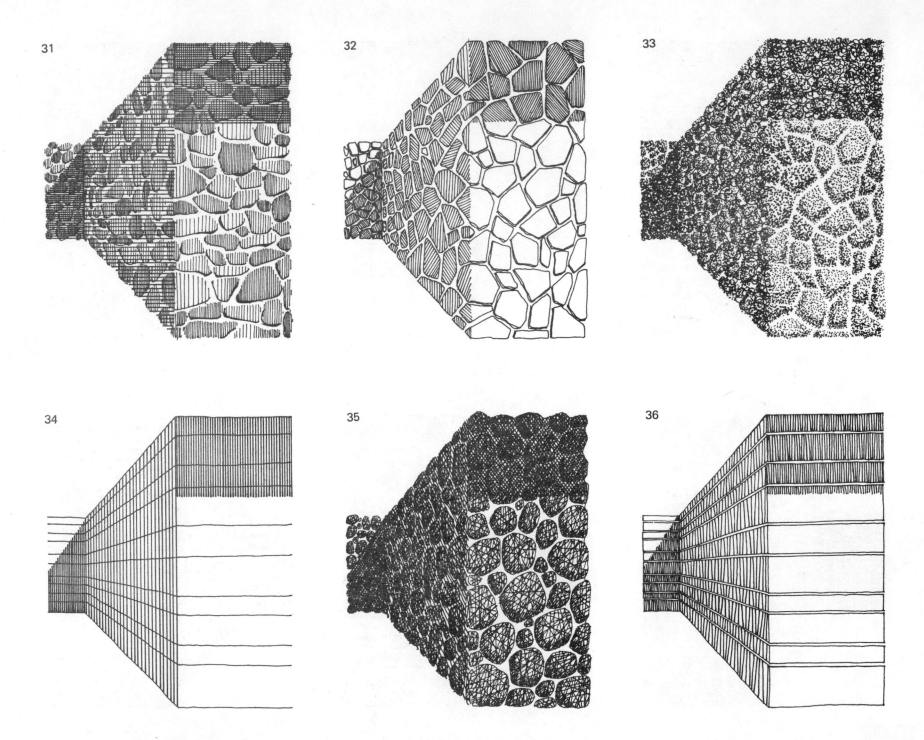

31 32 33

34 35 36

11

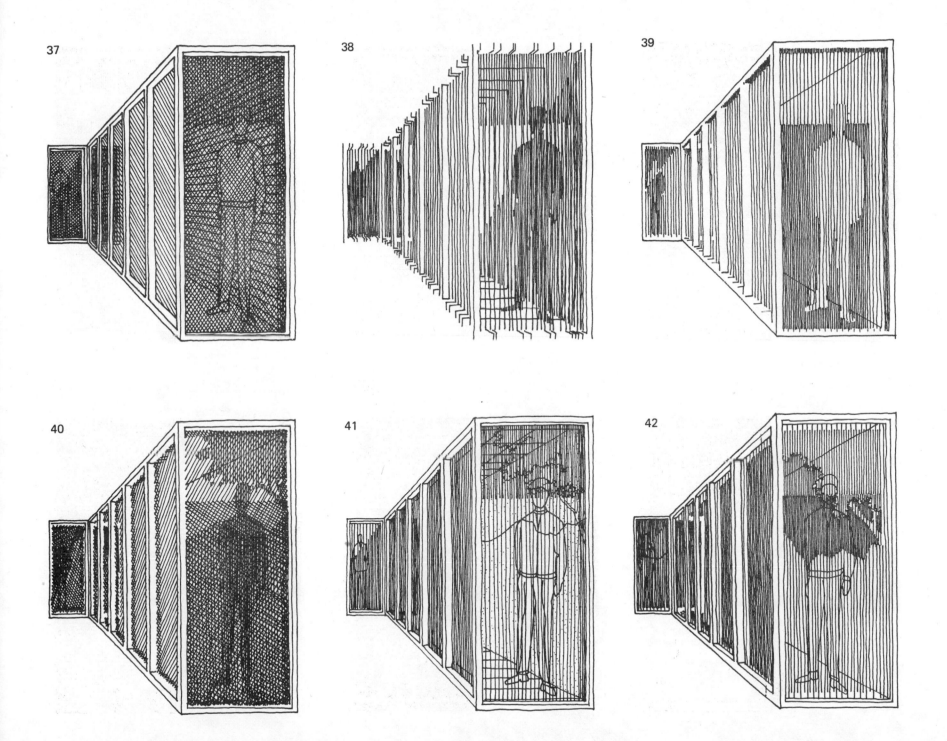

43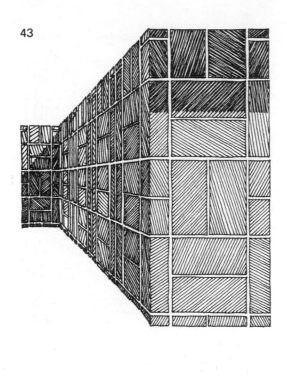

44

45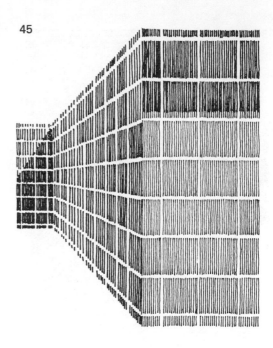

46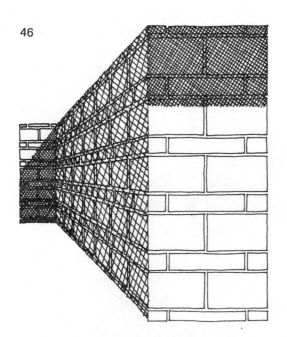

47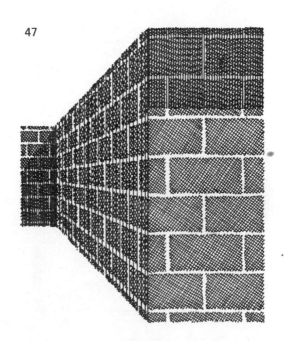

48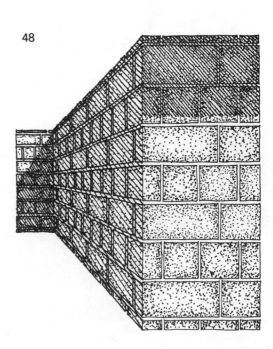

PAVING TEXTURES

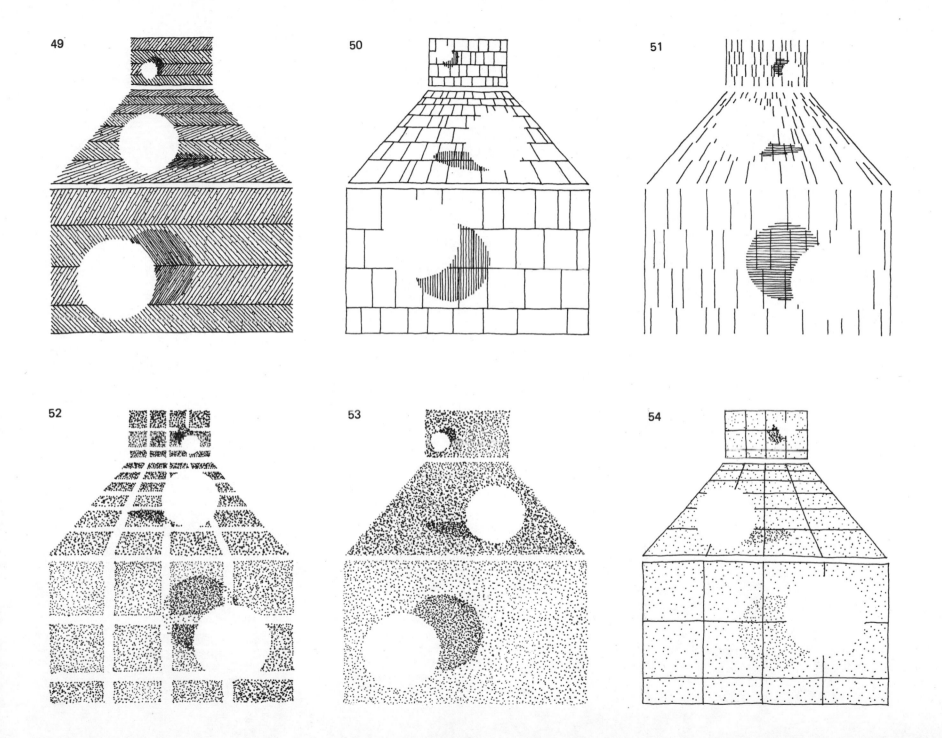

55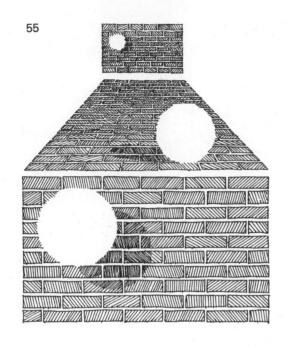

56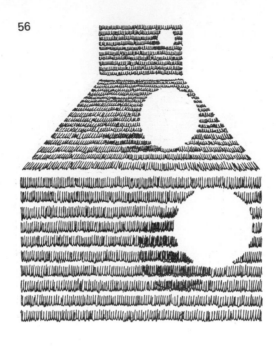

57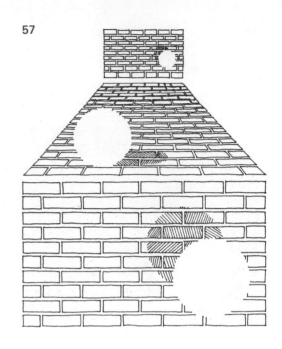

58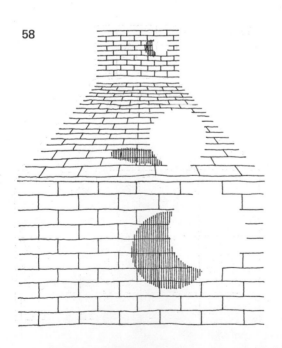

59

60

61

62
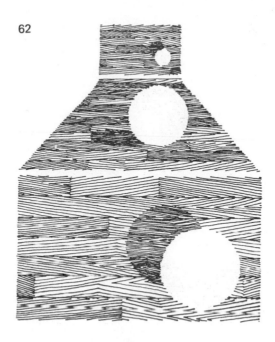

63

64
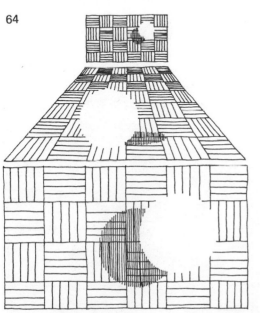

65
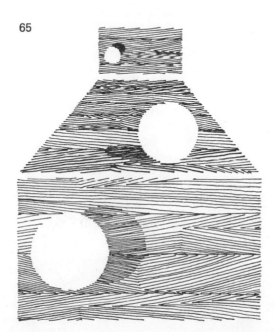

66
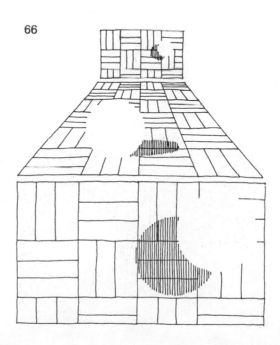

18

67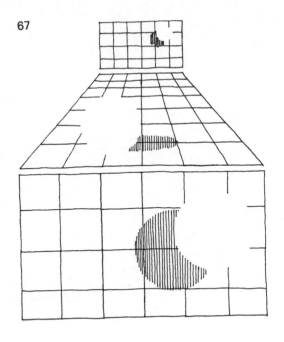

68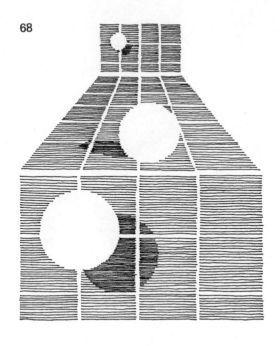

69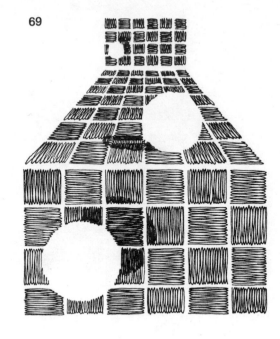

70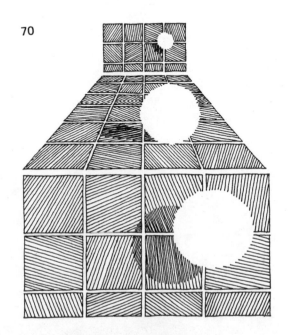

71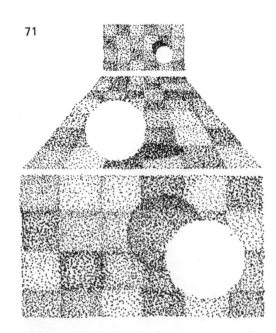

72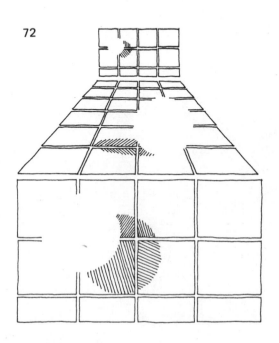

73

74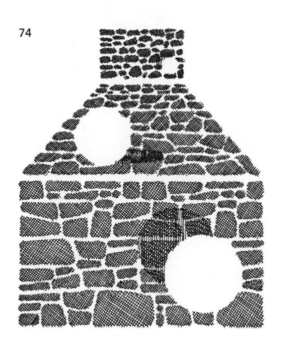

75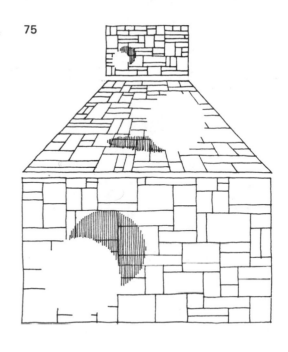

76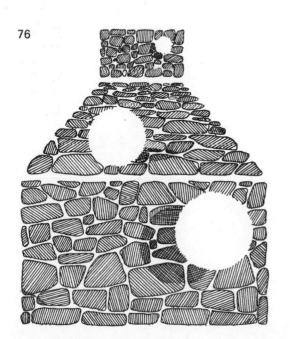

77

78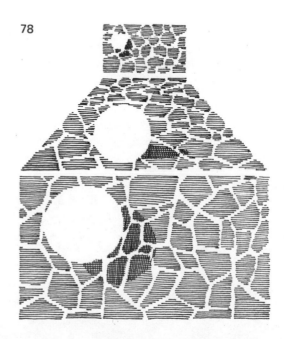

20

ROOFING TEXTURES

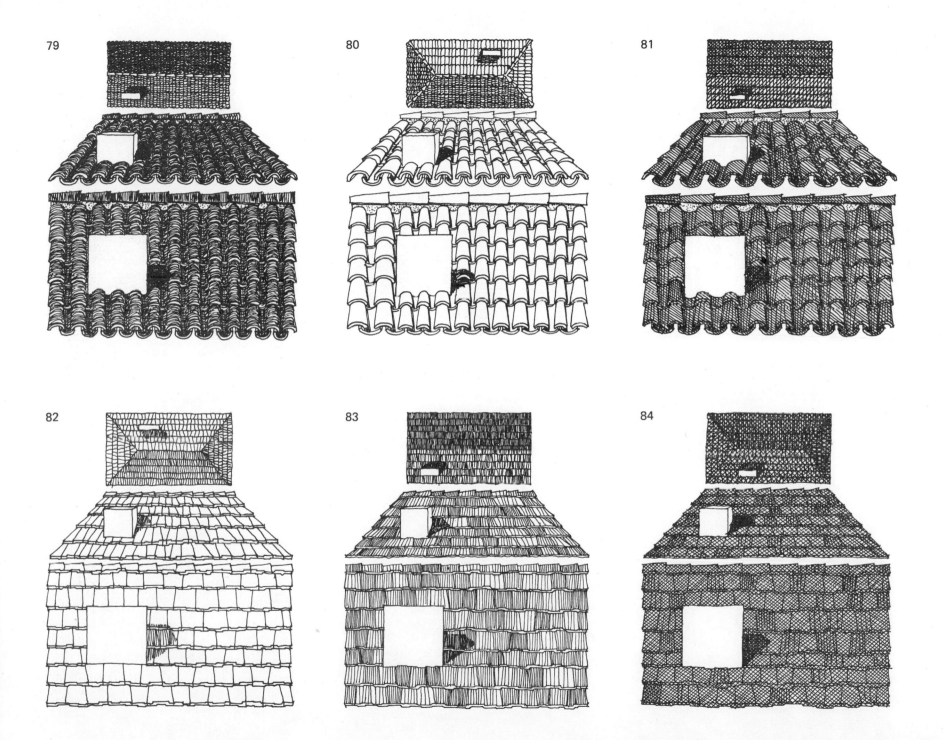

85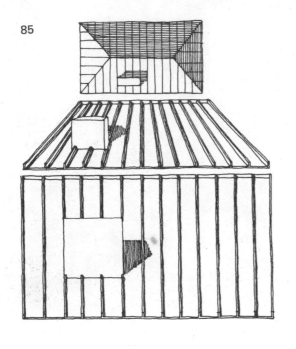

86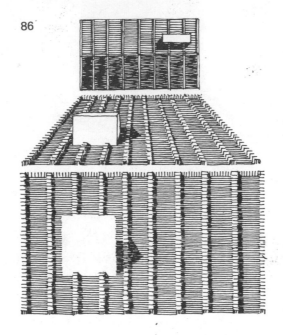

87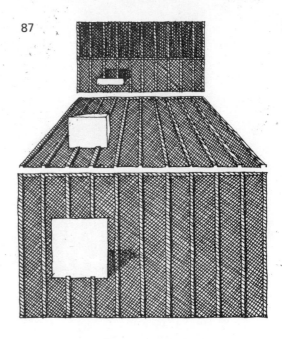

88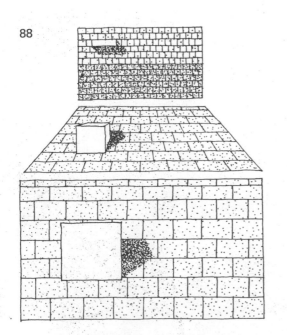

89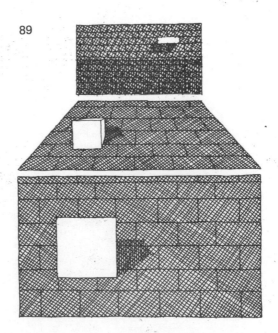

90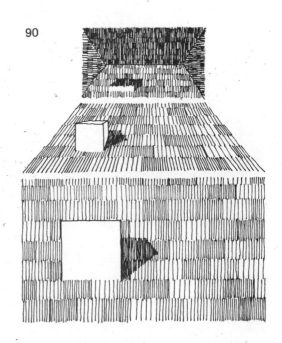

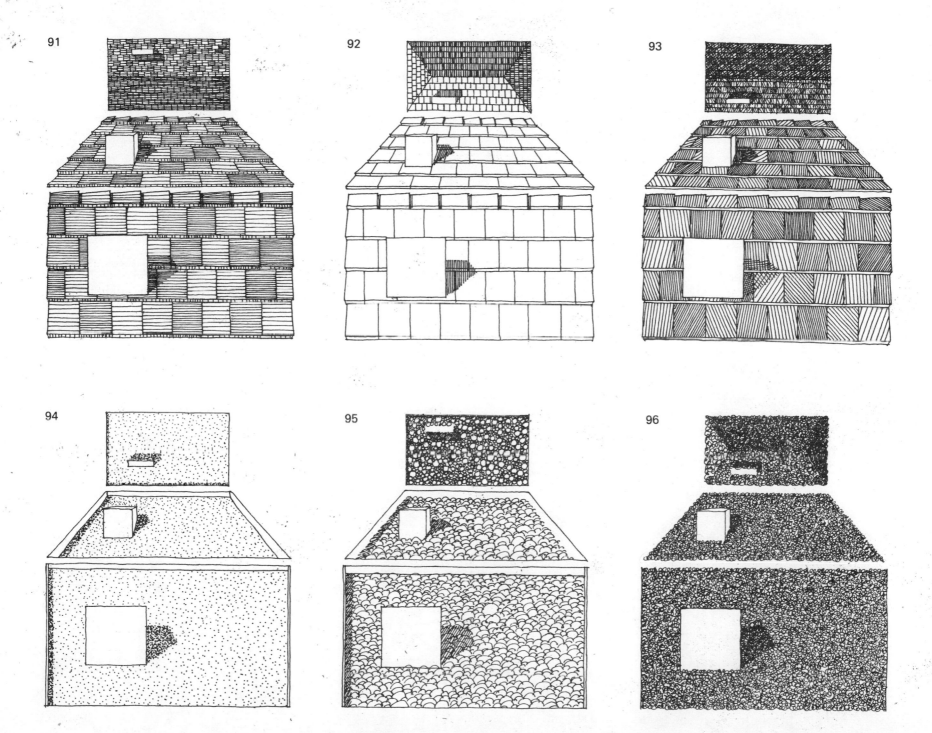

91

92

93

94

95

96

24

97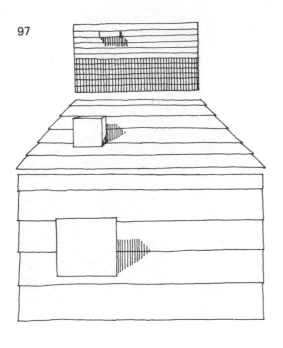

98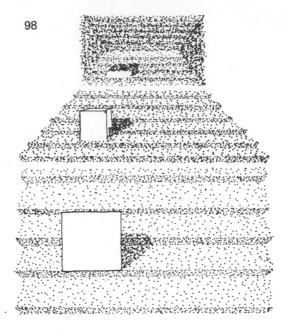

99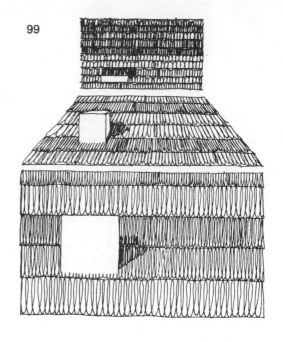

100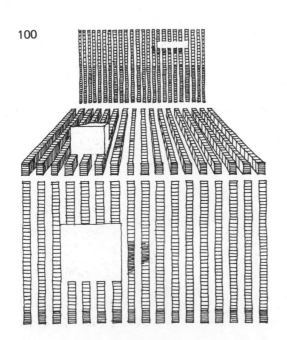

101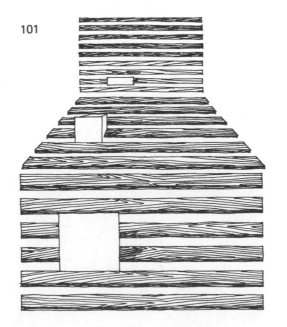

102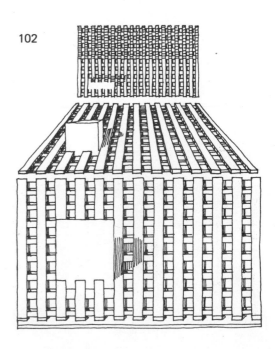

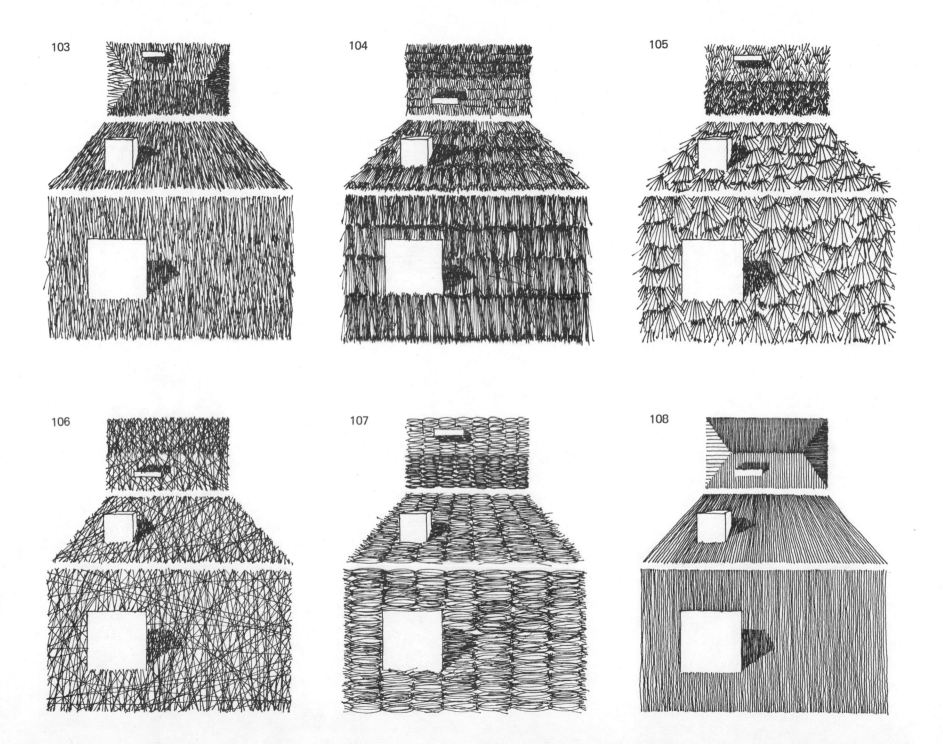

103 104 105

106 107 108

26

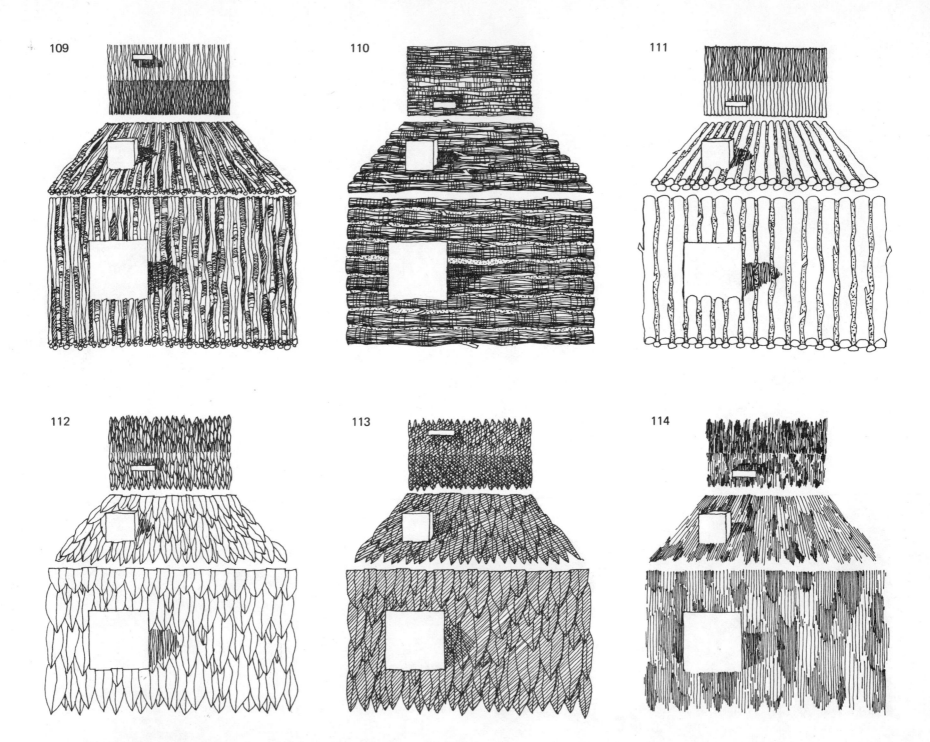

115

116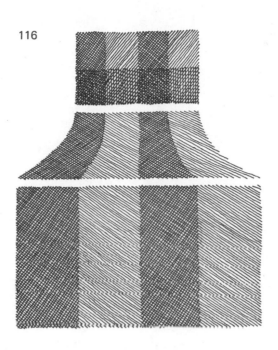

117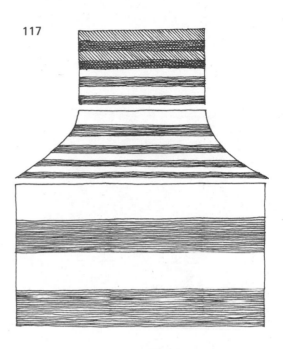

118

119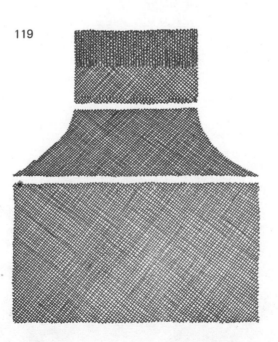

120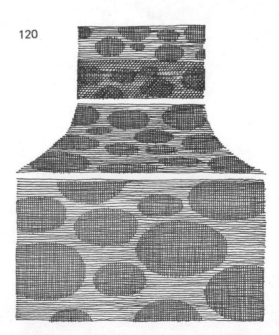

HUMAN FIGURES

121

122

123

124

125

126

127

128

129

31

130

131

132

133

134

135

136

137

138

139

140

141

142

143

144

145

146

147

148

32

149

150

151

152

153

154

155

156

157

158

33

159

160

161

162

163

164

165

166

167

168

169

170

171

172

173

174

175

176

177

178

179

180

181

182

183

184

185

186

36

199

200

201

202

203

204

205

206

207

208

209

210

211

212

213

214

215

216

217

218

219

220

221

222

223

224

225

226

227

228

229

230

231

232

233

234

235

236

237

238

239

240

241

242

243

244

245

246

247

248

249

250

251

252

41

FURNITURE

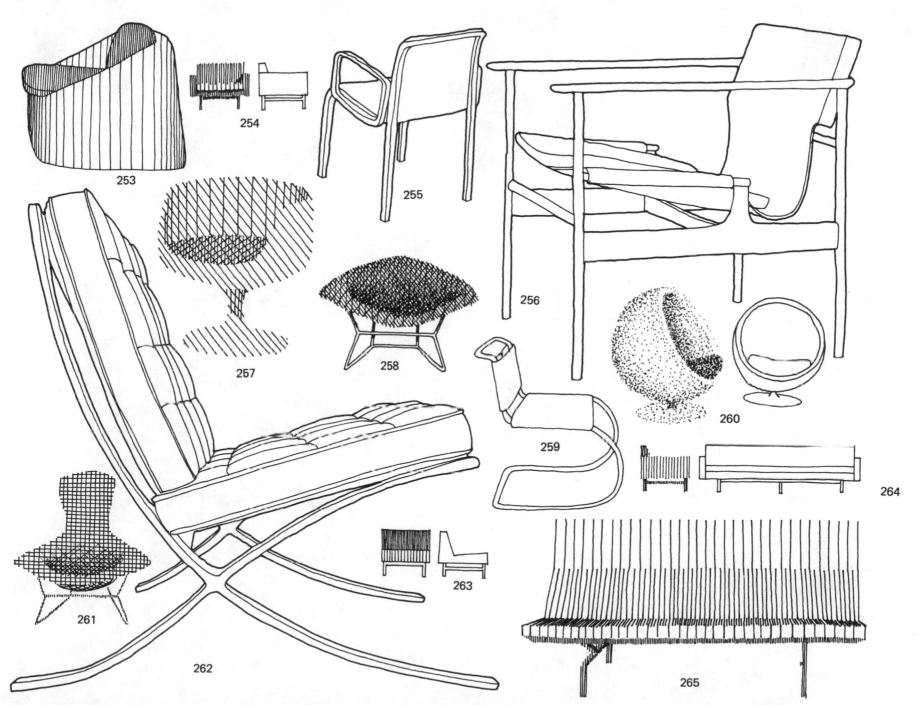

253

254

255

256

257

258

259

260

261

262

263

264

265

44

266

267

268

269

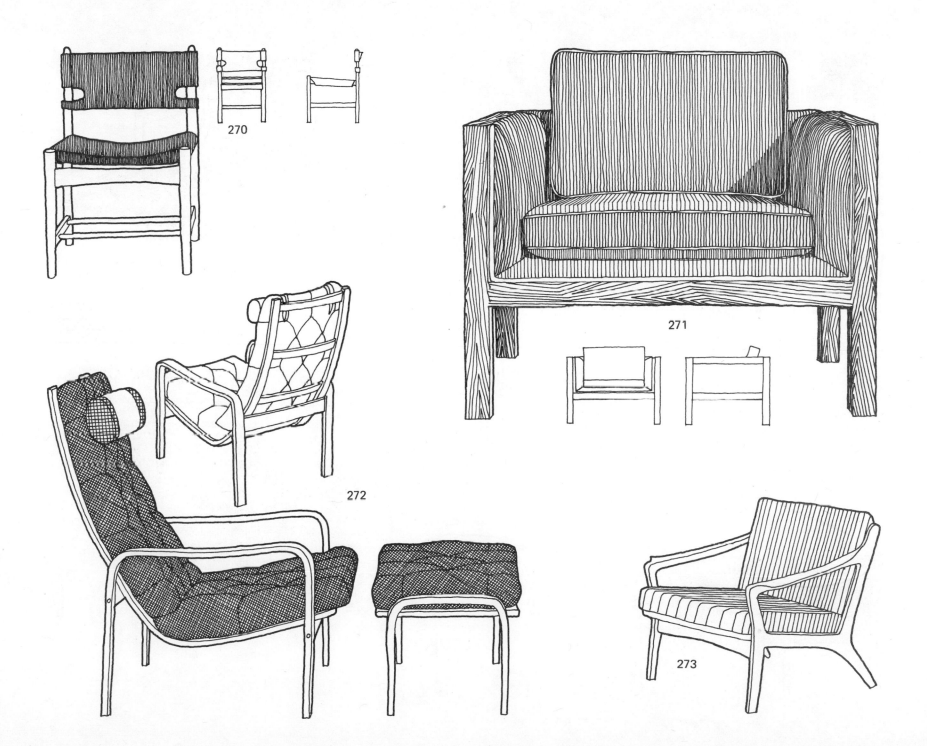

270

271

272

273

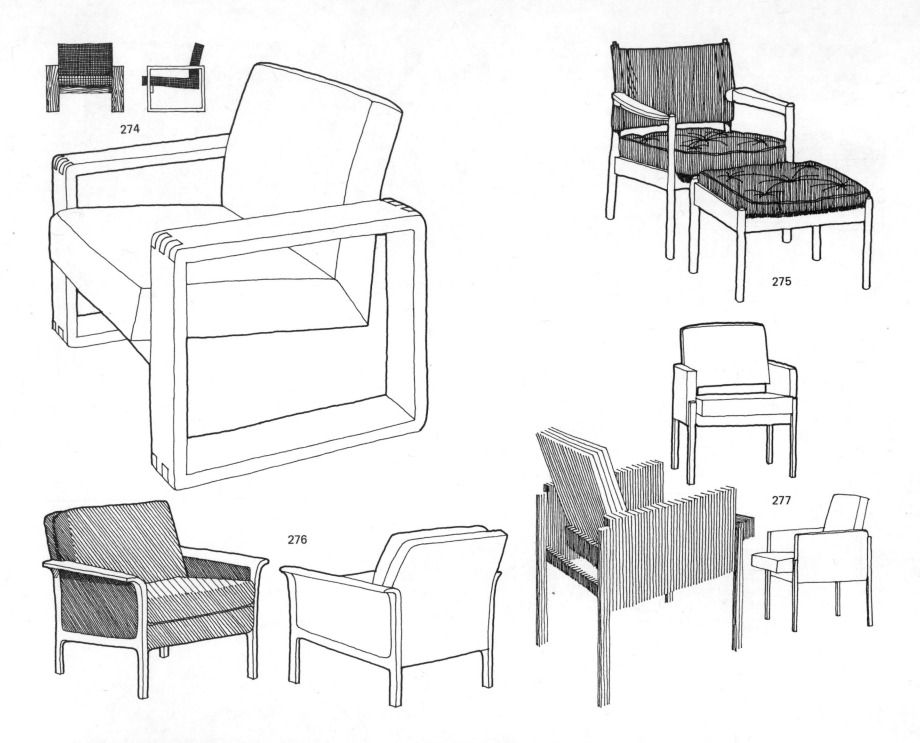

274

275

276

277

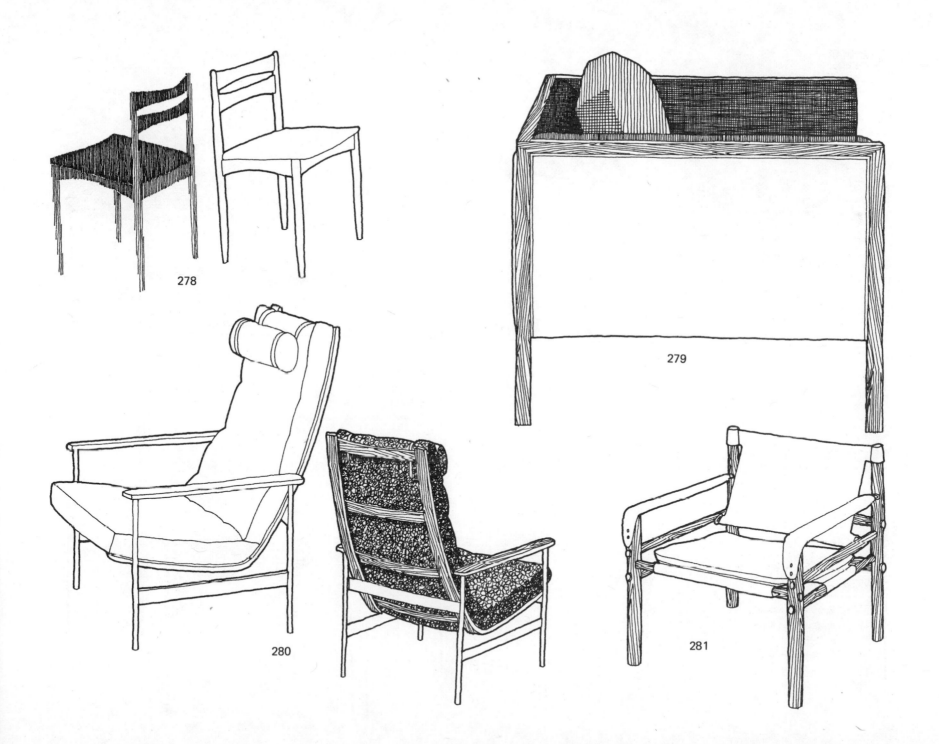

278

279

280

281

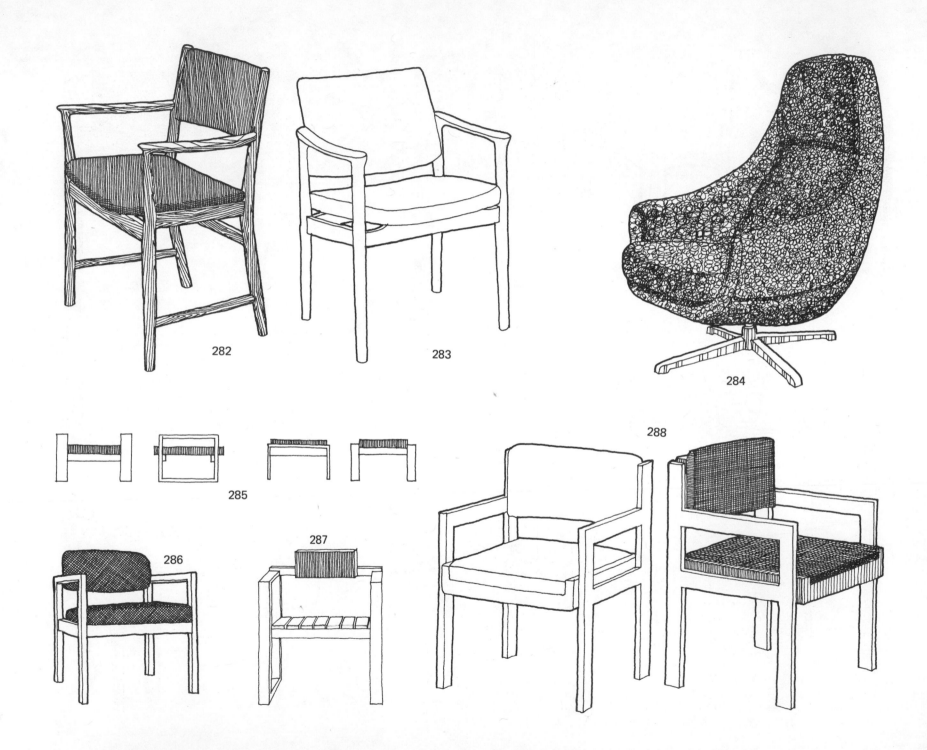

282

283

284

285

286

287

288

49

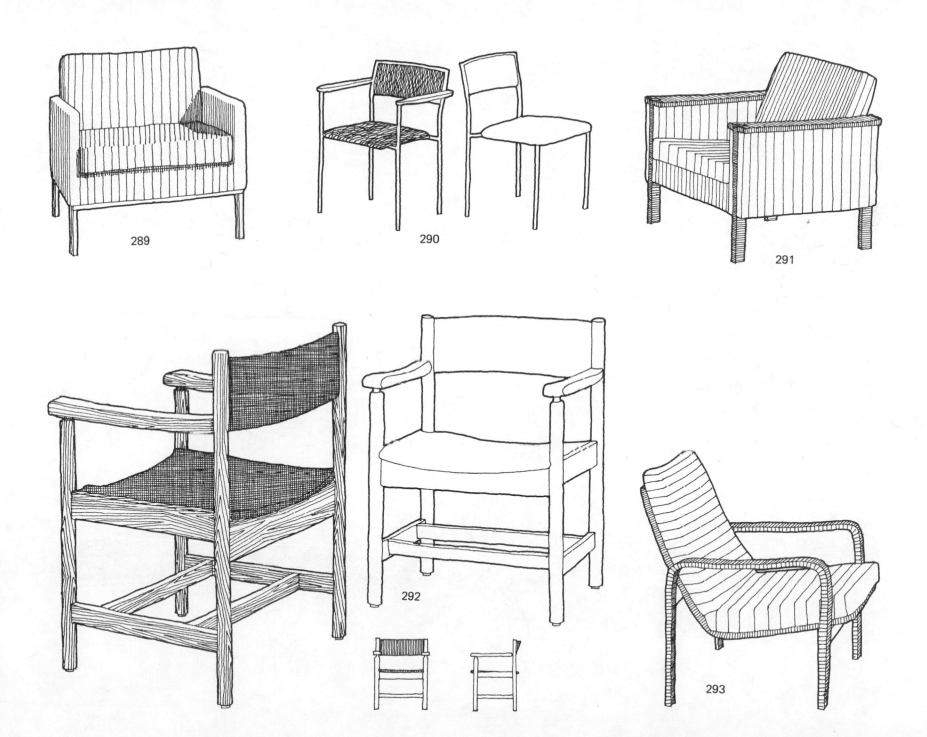

289

290

291

292

293

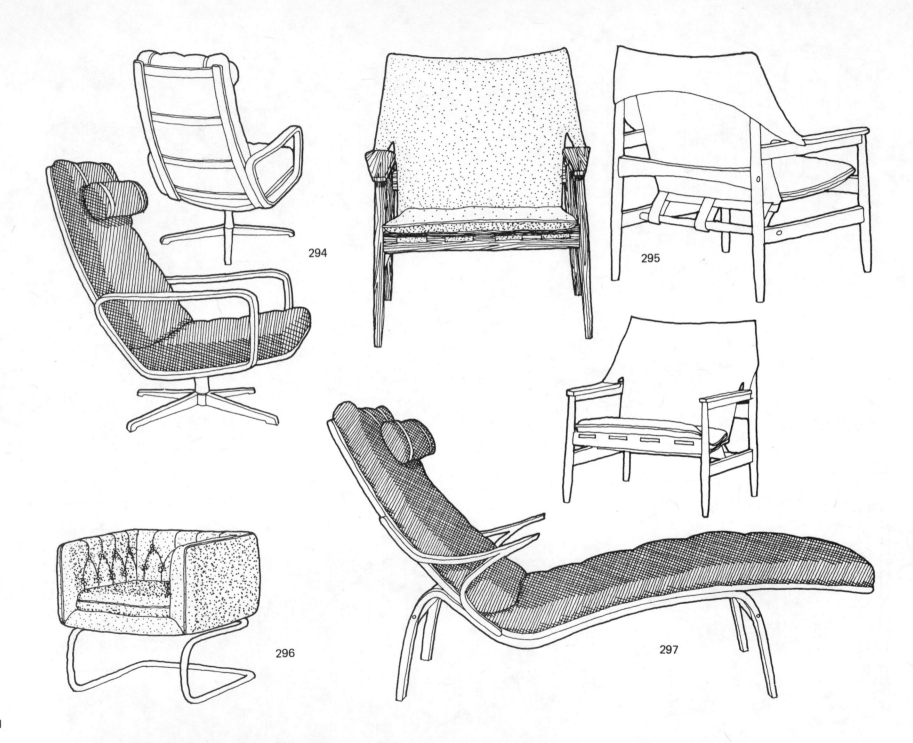

294

295

296

297

51

298

299

300

301

302

303

304

305

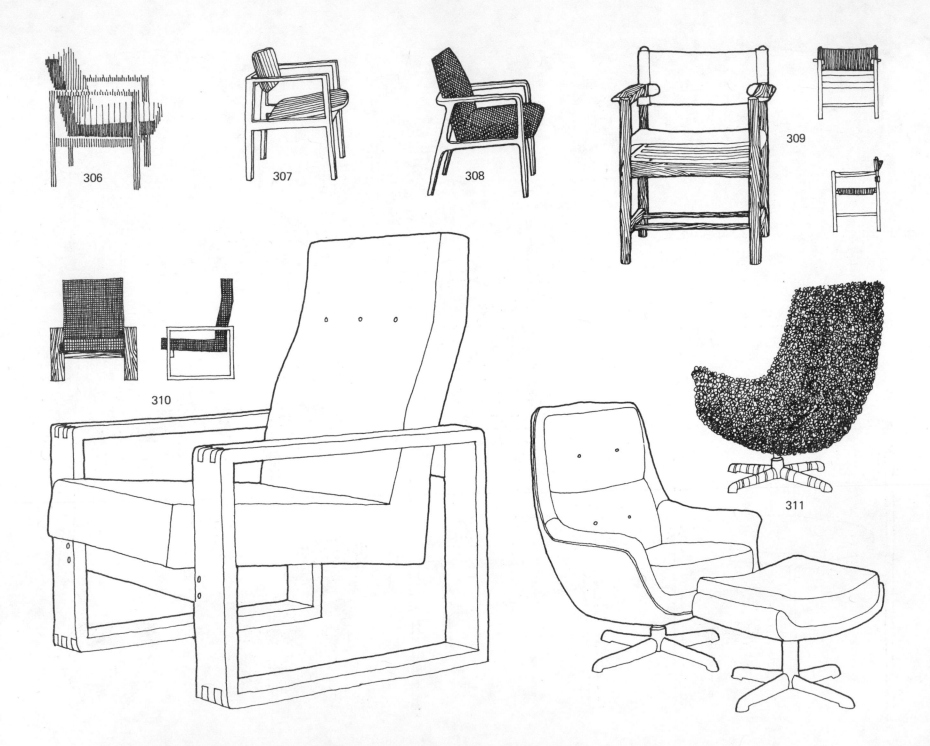

306

307

308

309

310

311

312

313

314

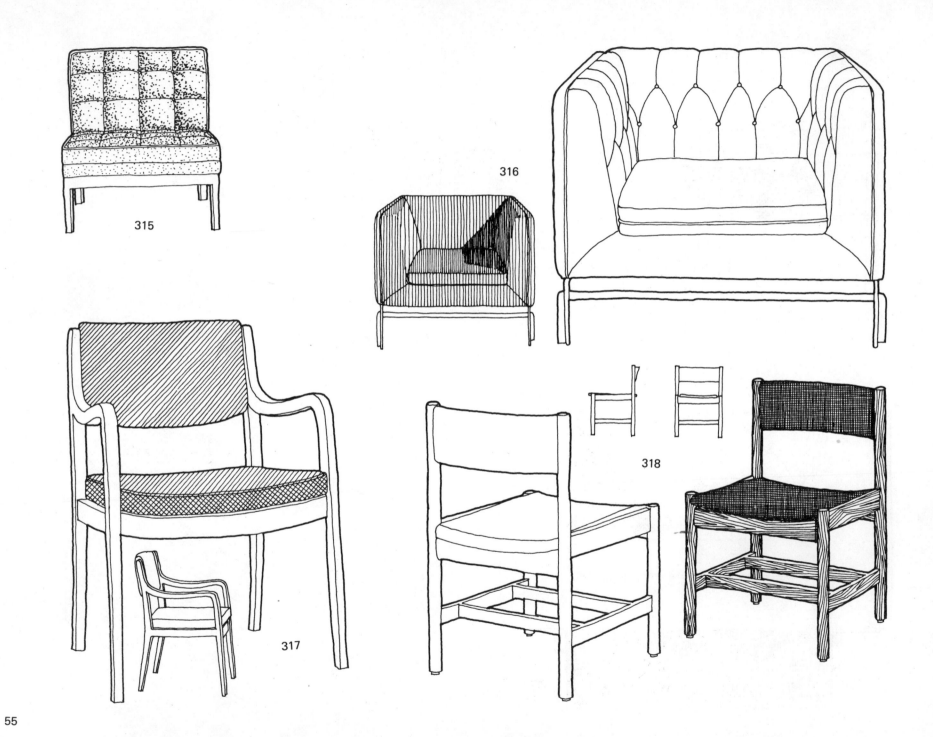

315

316

317

318

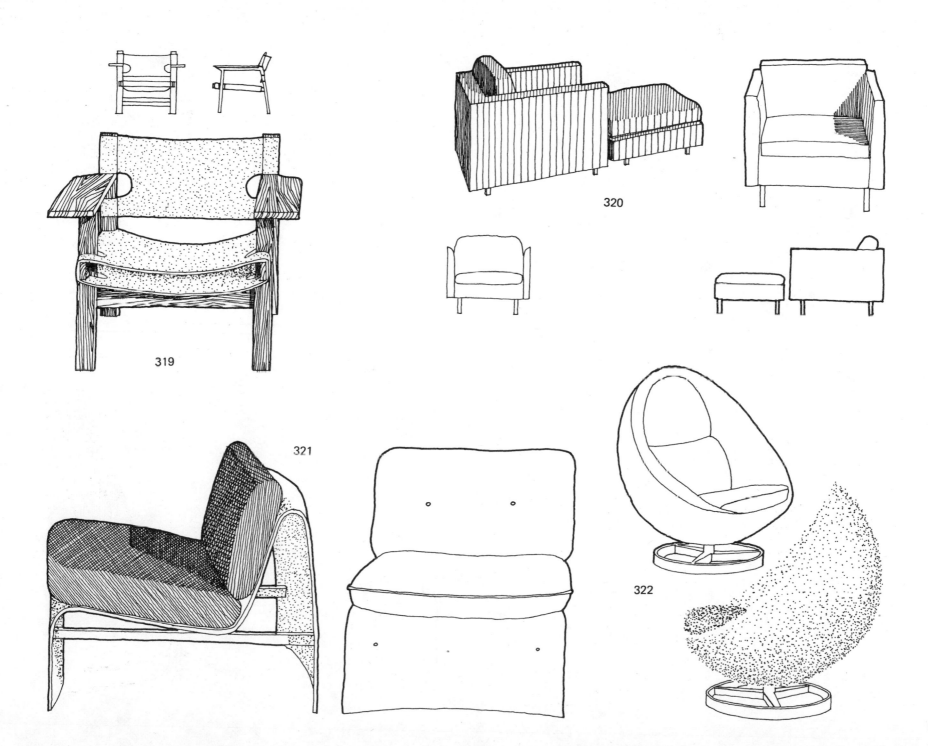

319

320

321

322

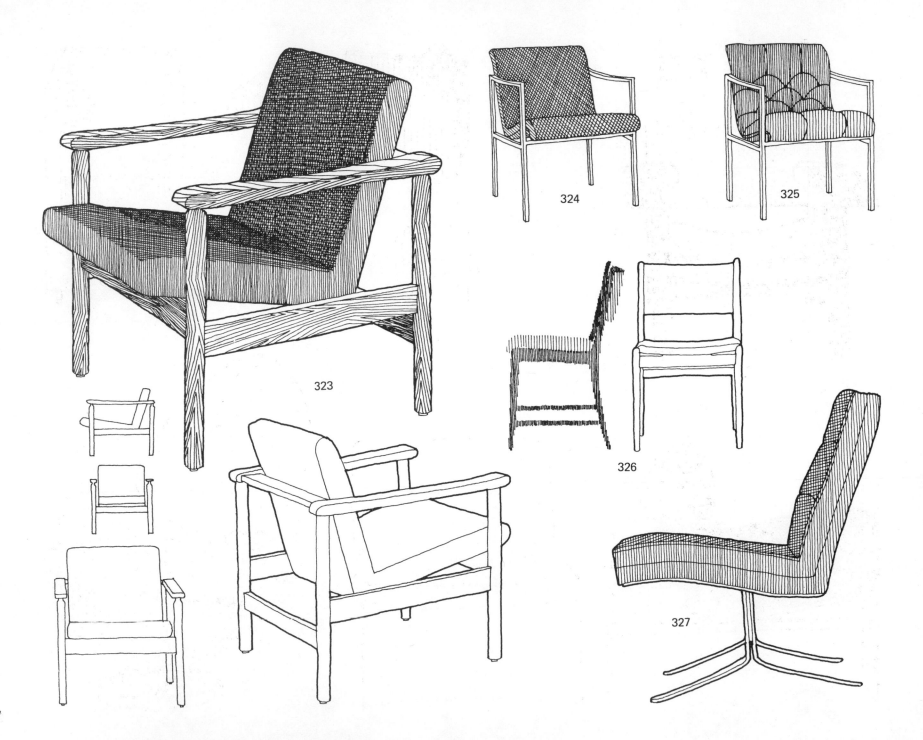

323

324

325

326

327

328

329

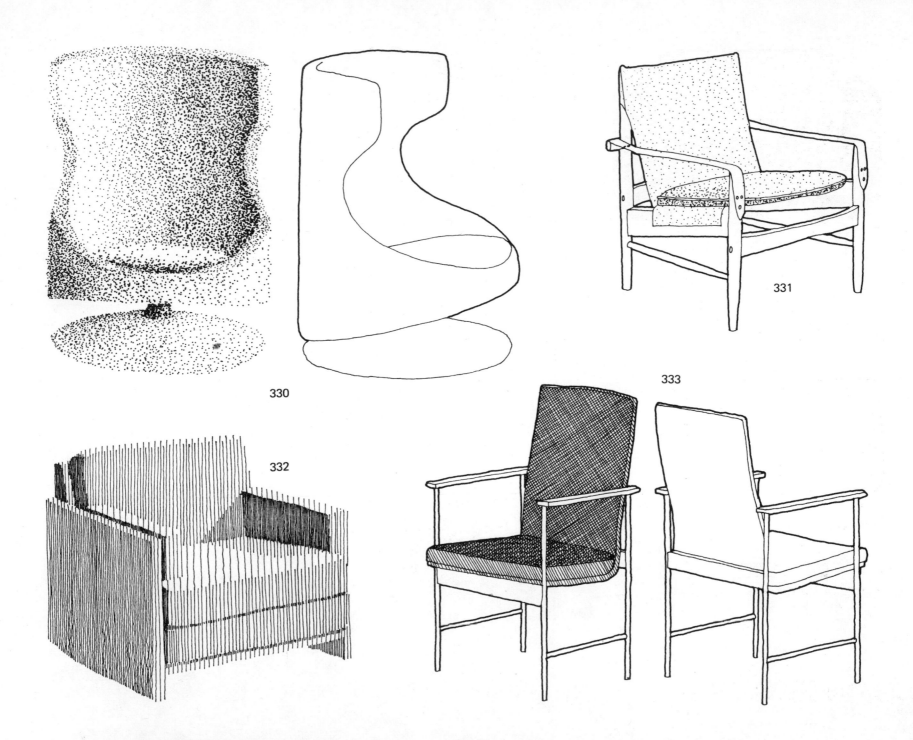

330

331

332

333

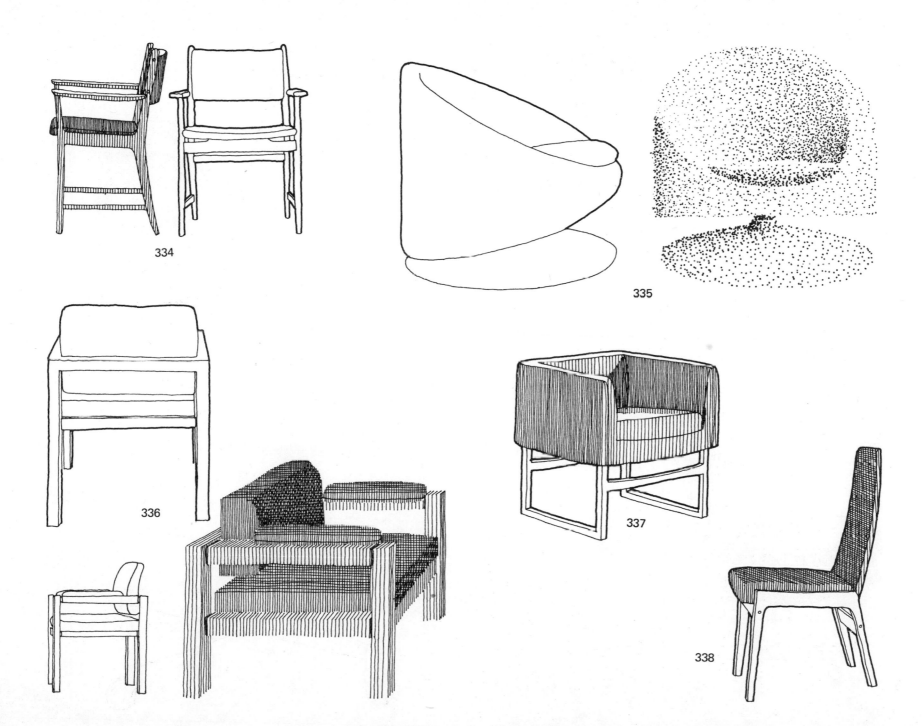

334

335

336

337

338

60

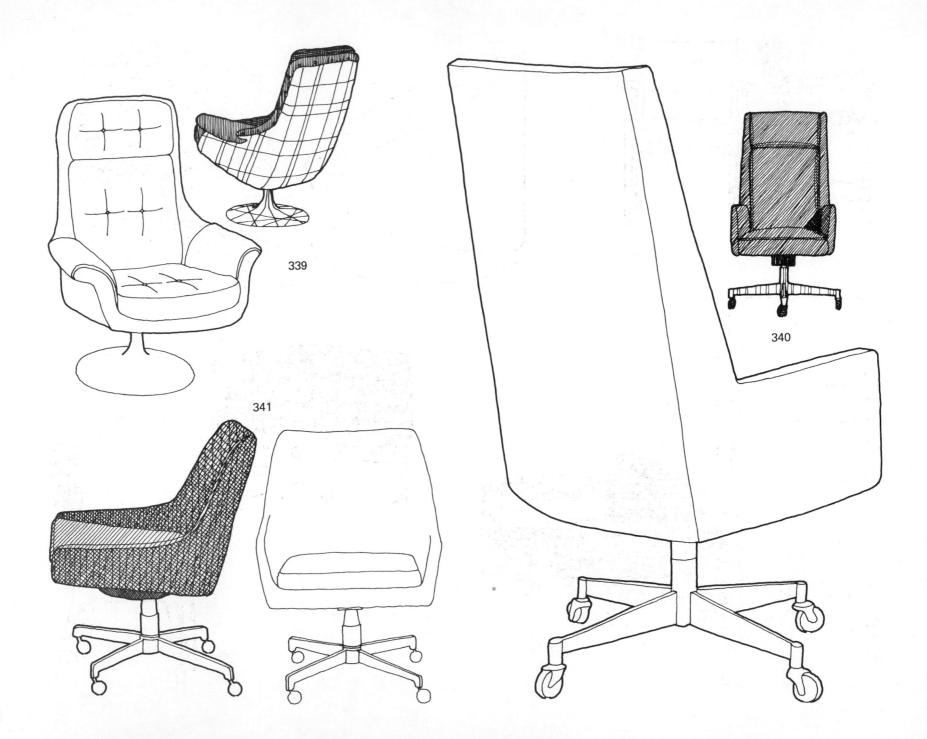

339

341

340

342

343

344

345

346

347

348

62

349

350

351

352

353

354

355

356

357

358

359

360

361

362

363

364

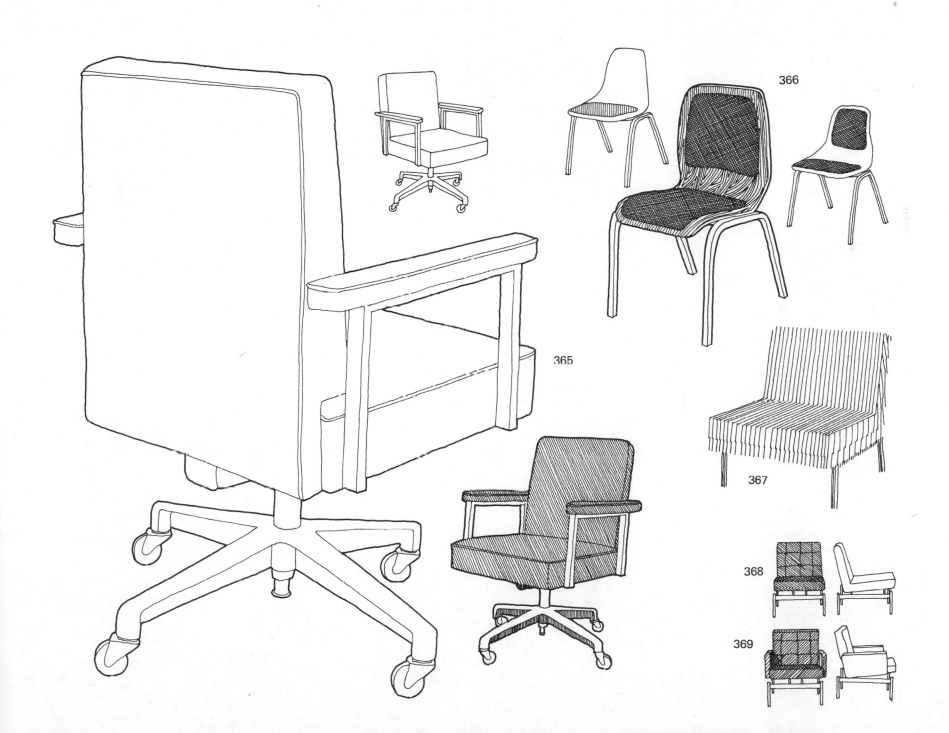

365

366

367

368

369

66

370

371

372

373

374

375

376

377

378

379

380

381

382

383

384

385

69

386

387

388

389

390

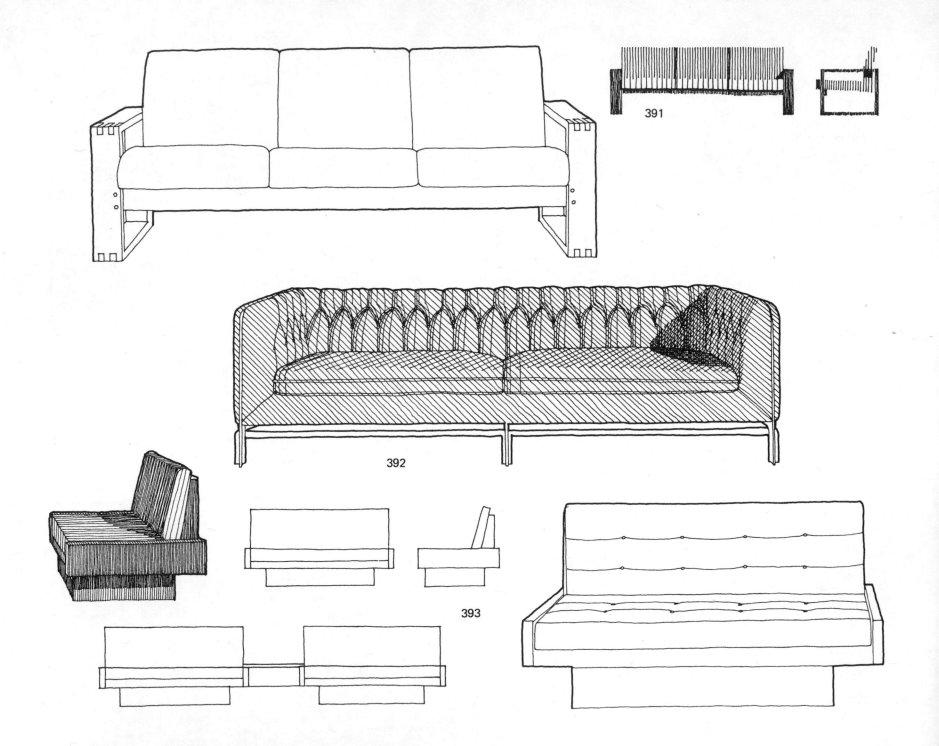

391

392

393

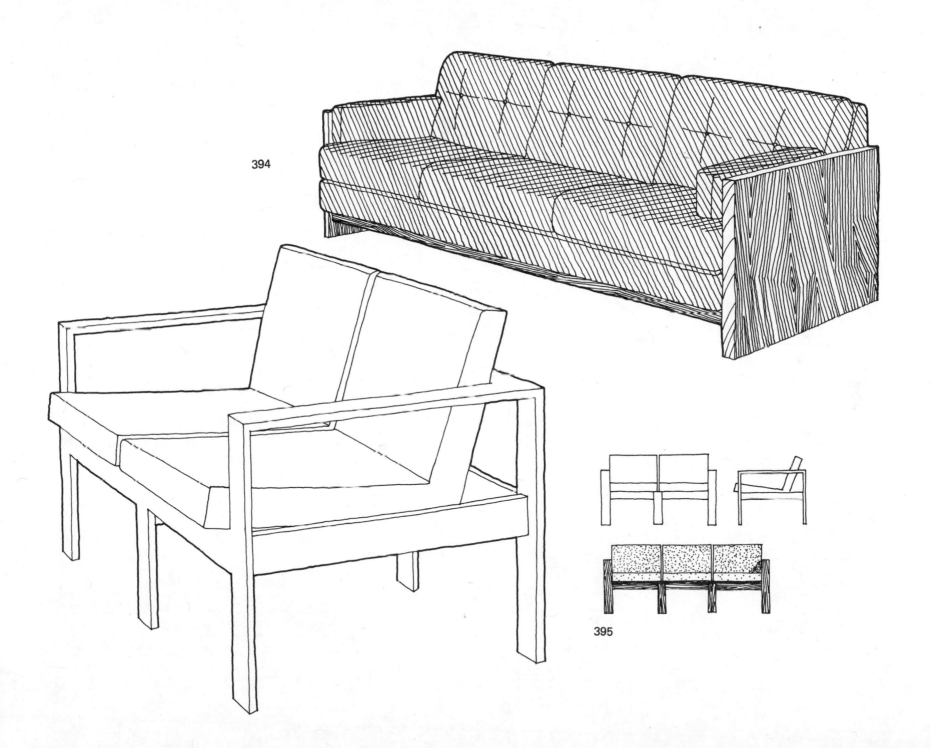

394

395

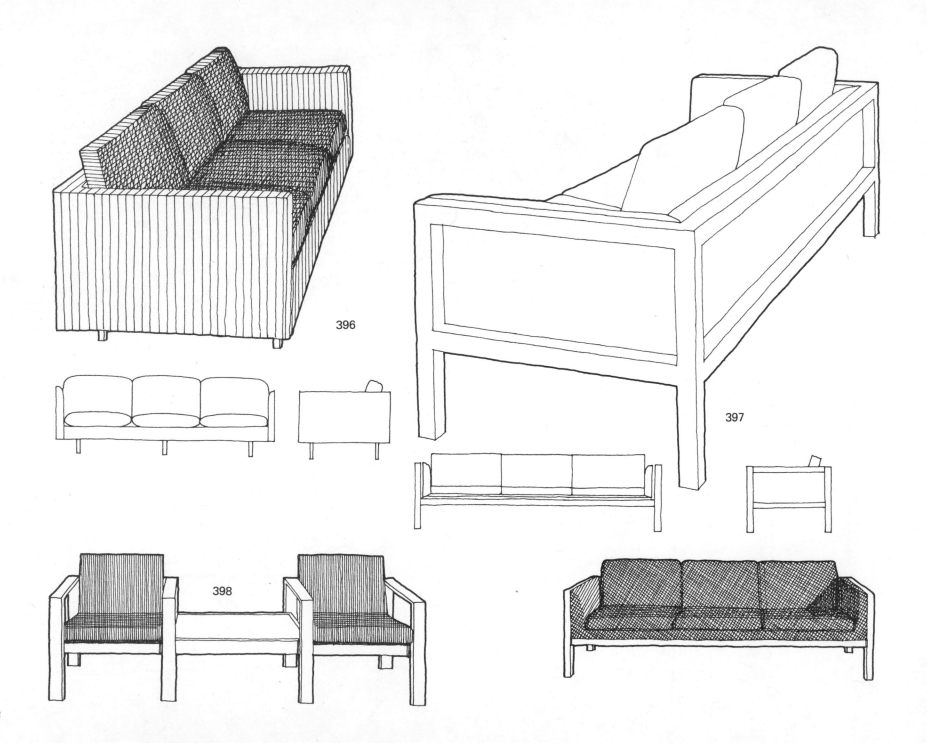

396

397

398

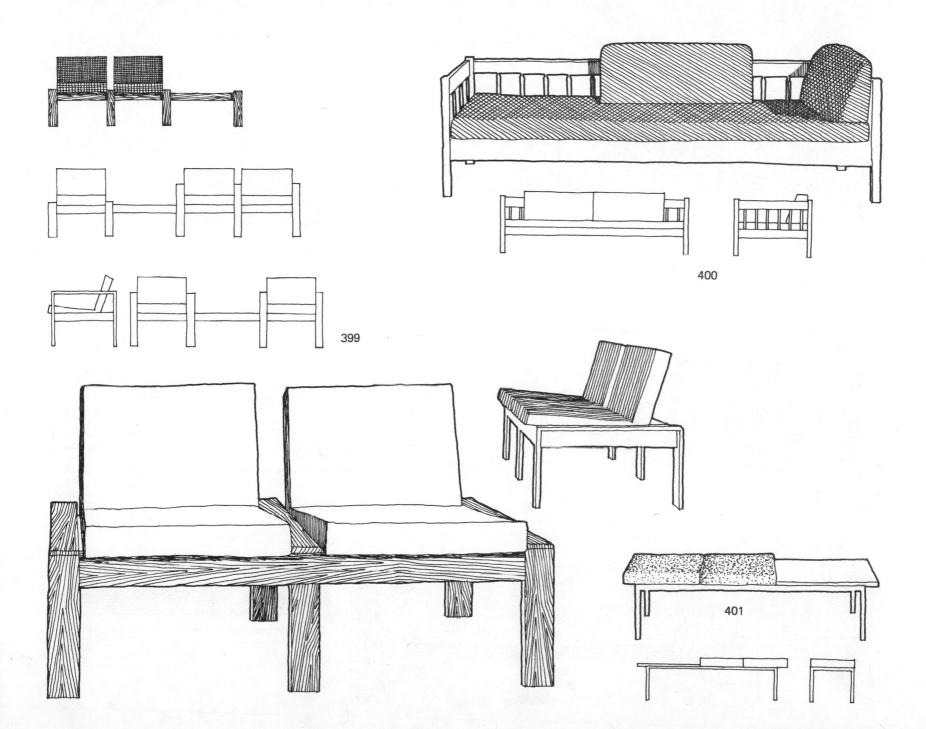

399

400

401

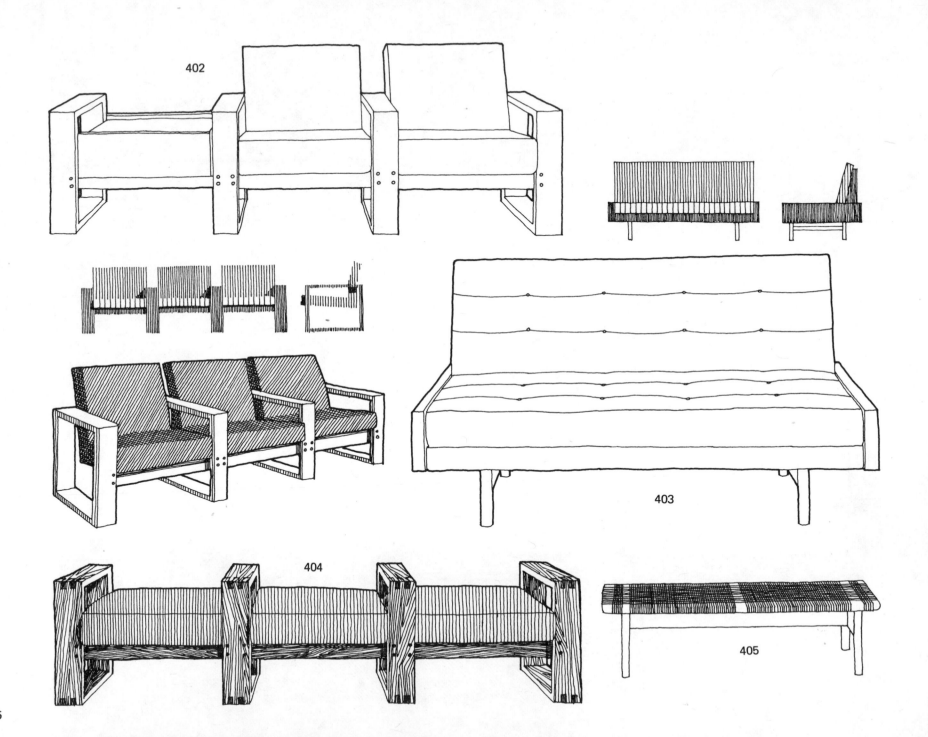

402

403

404

405

406

407

408

409

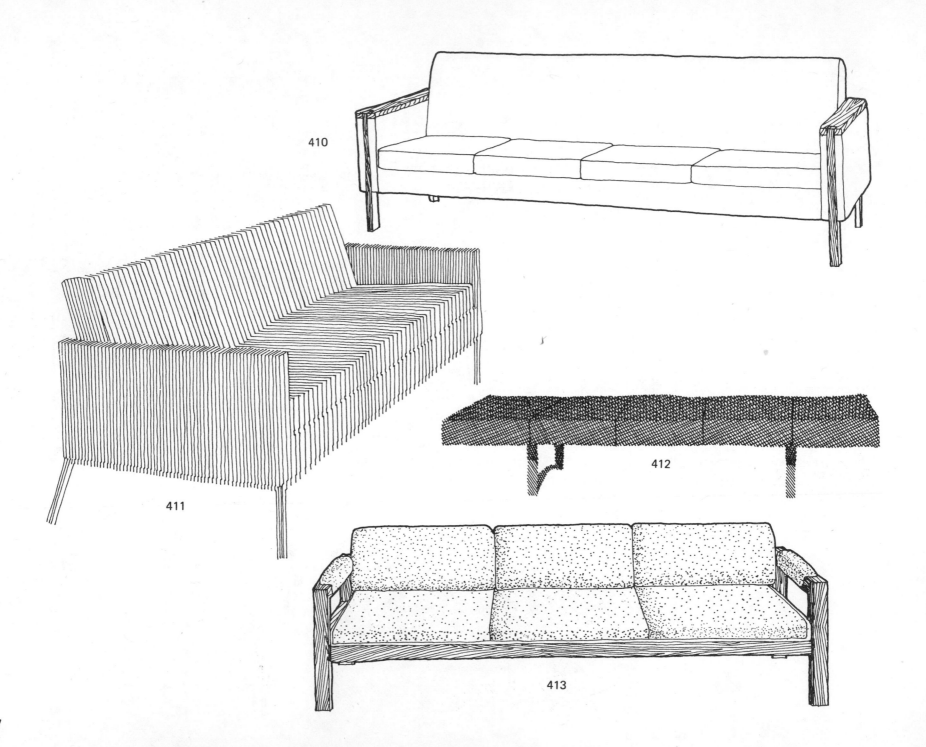

410

411

412

413

414

415

416

417

418

420

419

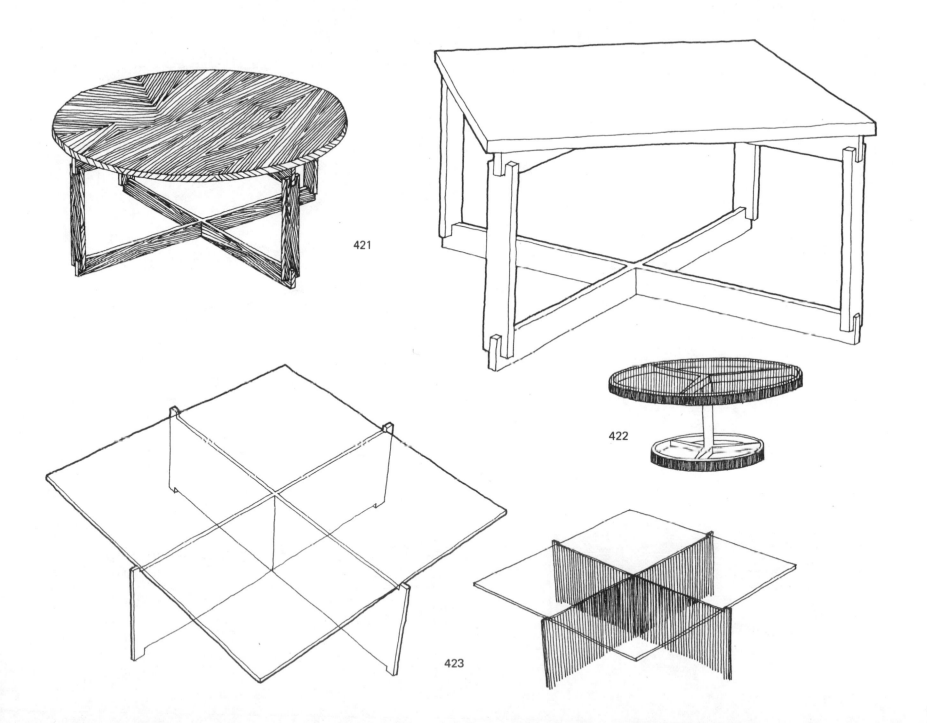

421

422

423

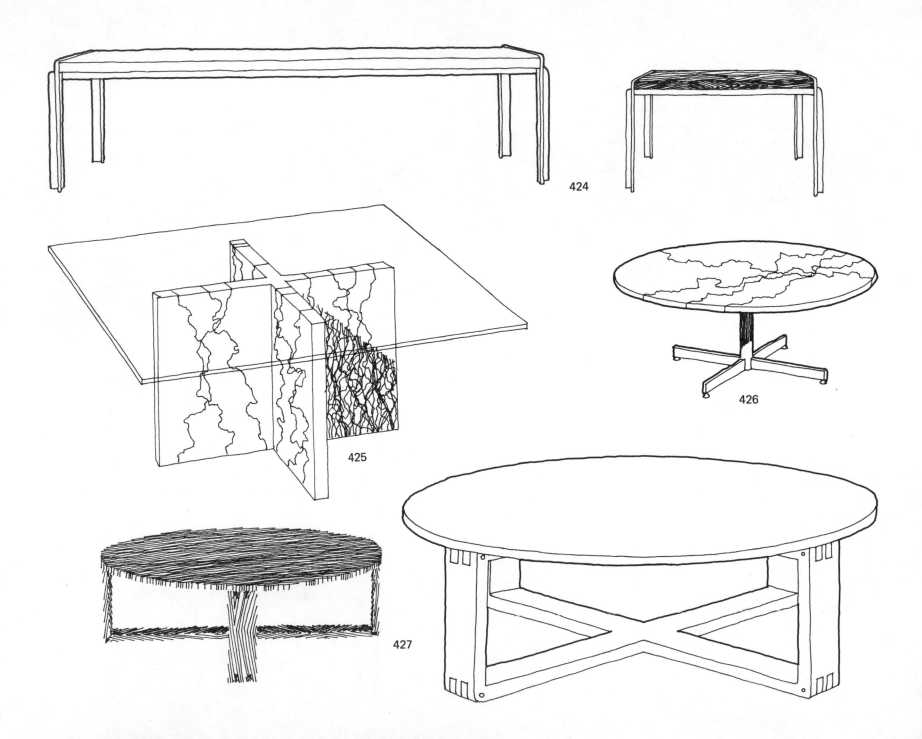

424

425

426

427

428

429

430

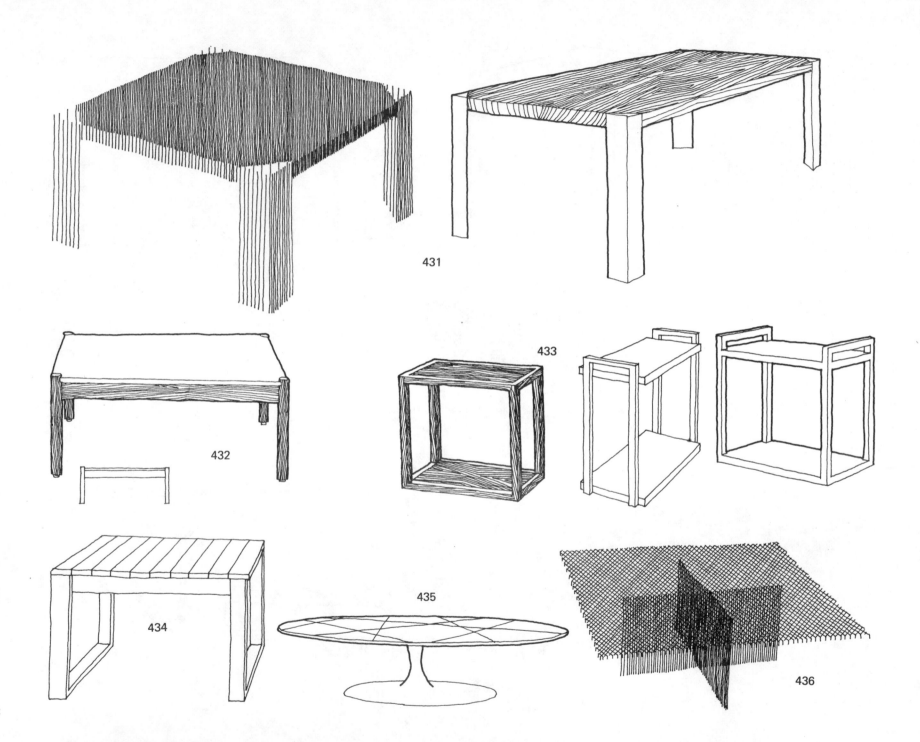

431

433

432

434

435

436

83

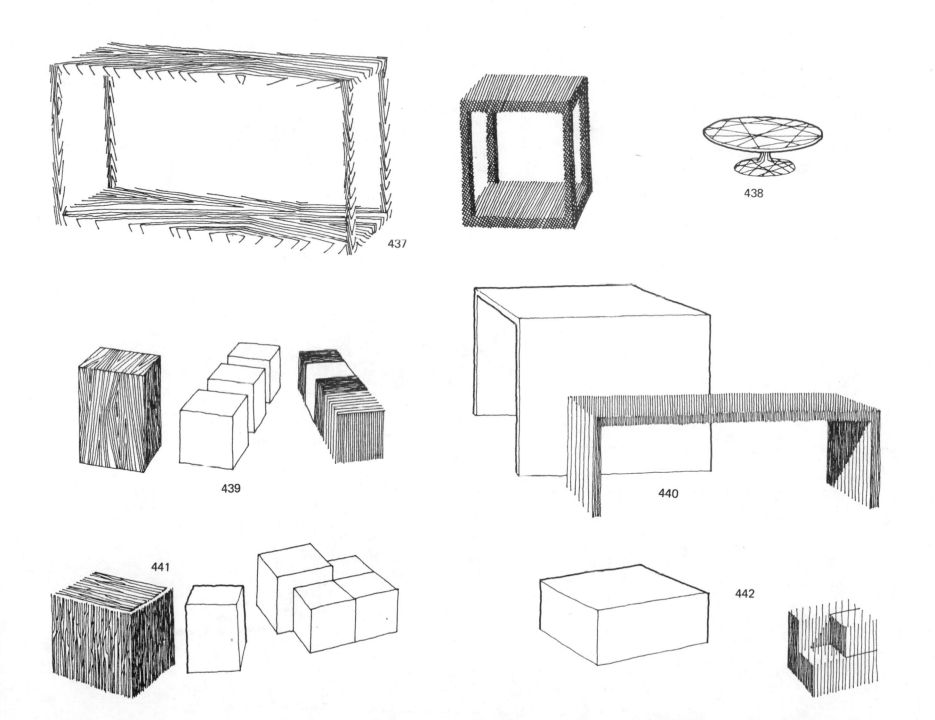

437

438

439

440

441

442

84

443

444

445

446

447

448

449

450

451

452

453

454

455

456

457

458

459

460

461

462

463

464

465

466

467

468

469

470

471

472

473

474

475

476

477

478

479

480

481

482

94

483

484

485

486

487

488

489

ACCESSORIES

490

491

492

493

494

495

496

497

498

499

500

501

502

503

504

505

506

507

508

509

510

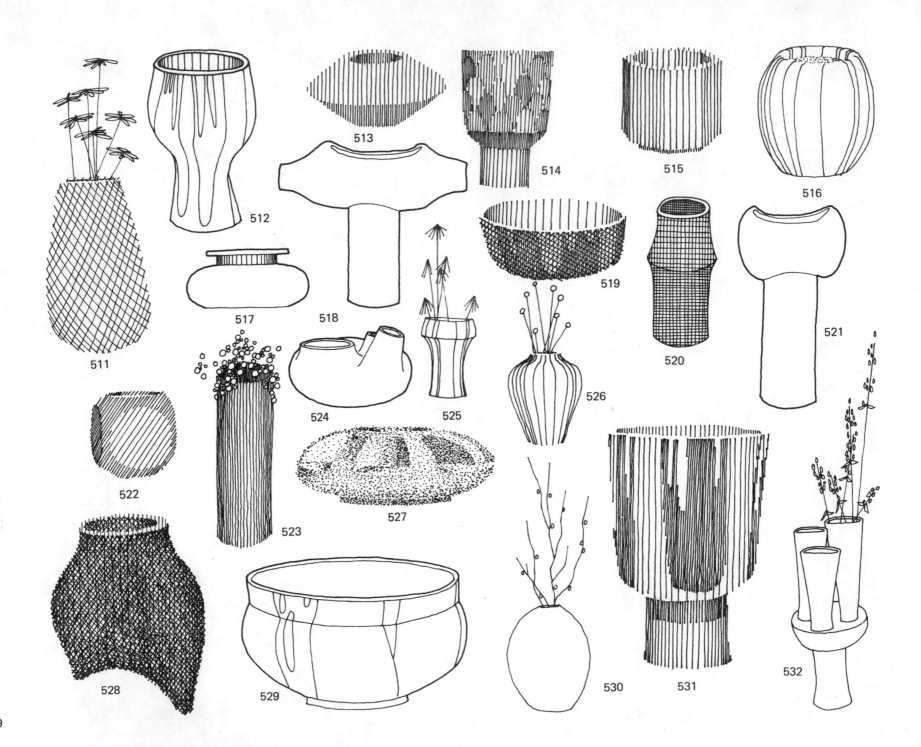

511

512

513

514

515

516

517

518

519

520

521

522

523

524

525

526

527

528

529

530

531

532

533

534

535

536

537

538

539

540

541

542

543

544

545

546

547

548

549

550

551

552

553

554

555

556

557

558

559

560

561

101

AUTOMOBILES

562

563

564

565

566

567

568

569

570

571

572

573

574

575

576

577

578

579

580

581

582

583

584

585

586

587

588

589

590

591

592

593

594

595

596

597

598

599

600

601

602

603

604

605

606

607

608

609

610

611

612

613

614

615

616

617

618

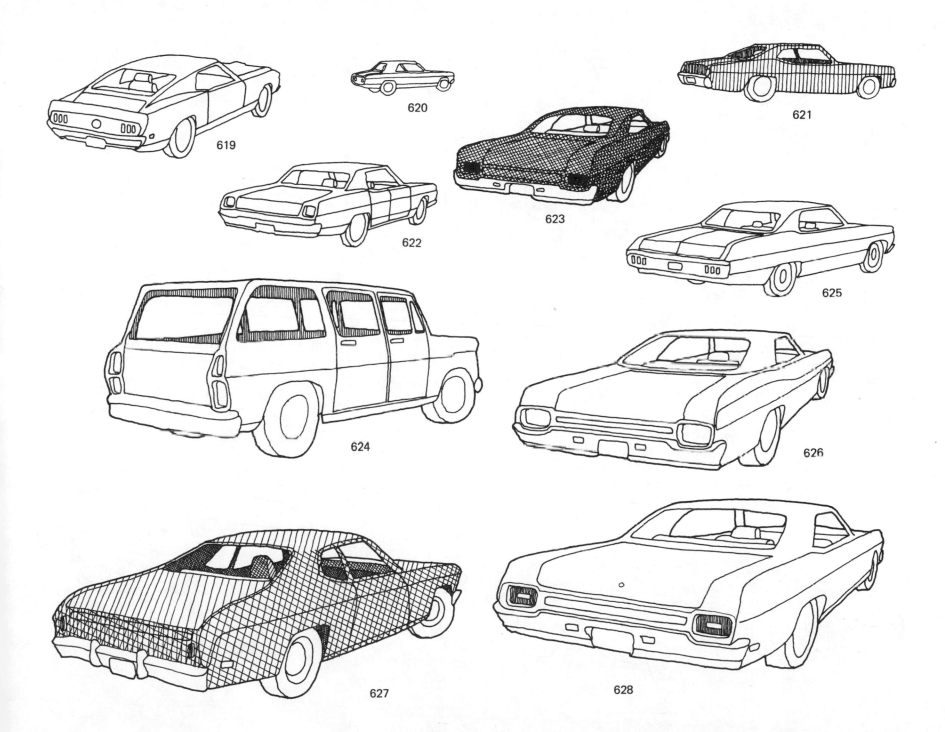

619

620

621

622

623

624

625

626

627

628

629

630

631

632

633

634

635

636

637

638

639

640

641

642

643

644

645

646

647

648

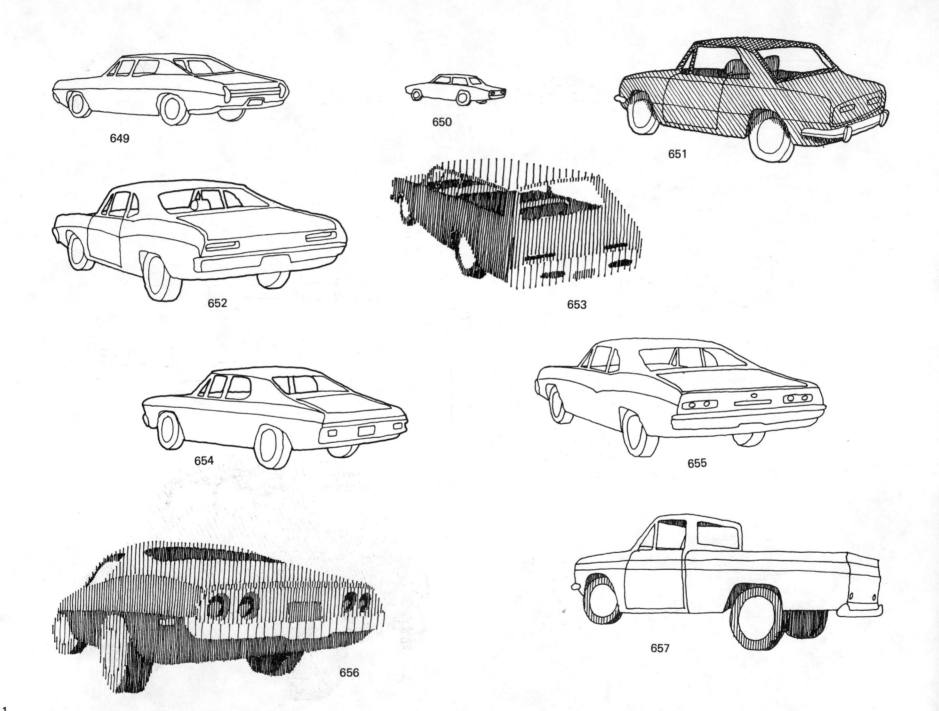

649

650

651

652

653

654

655

656

657

658

659

660

661

662

663

664

665

666

667

668

669

670

671

672

673

674

675

676

677

678

679

680

681

682

683

684

685

686

687

688

689

690

691

114

692

693

694

695

696

697

698

699

700

701

702

703

704

705

706

707

GROUND TEXTURES

708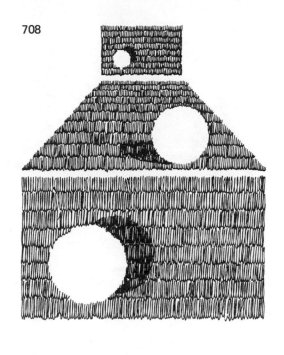

709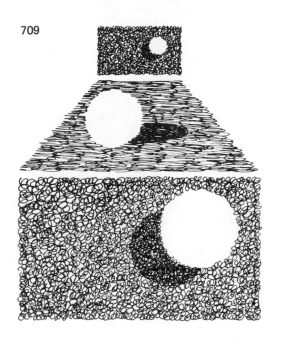

710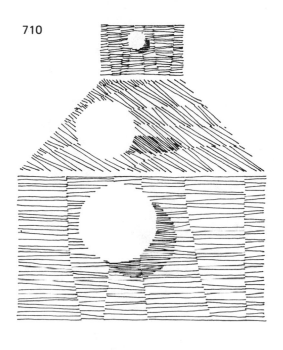

711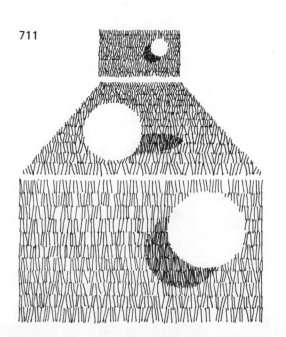

712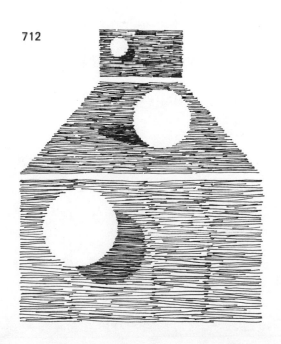

713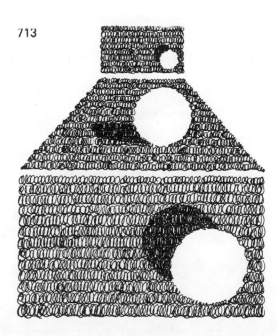

118

714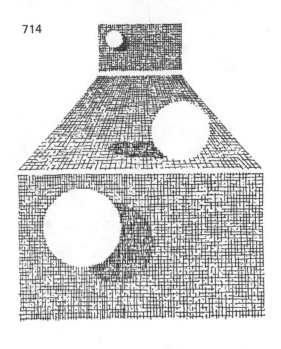

715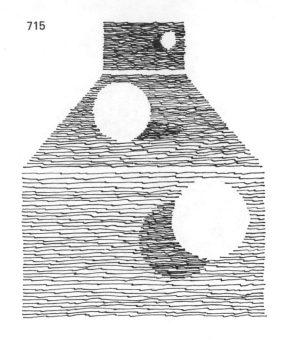

716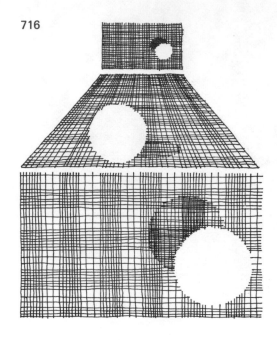

717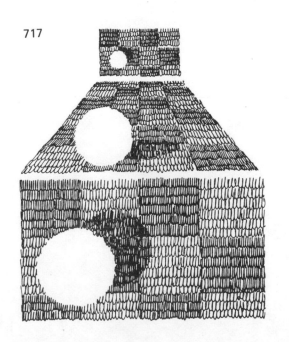

718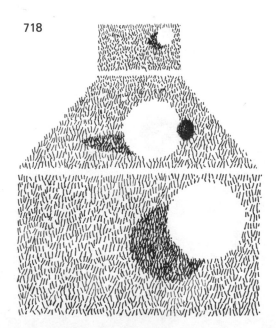

719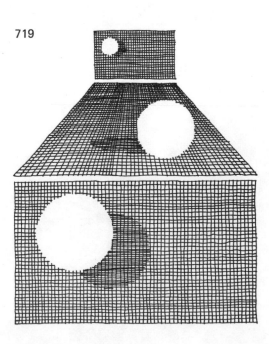

119

720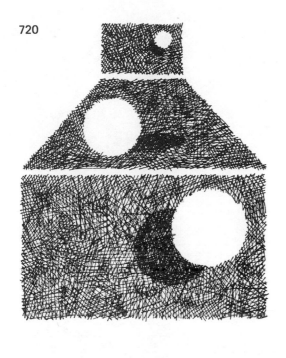

721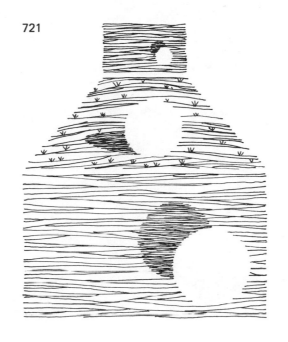

722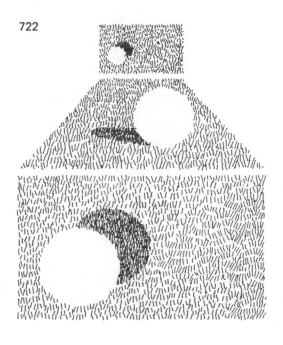

723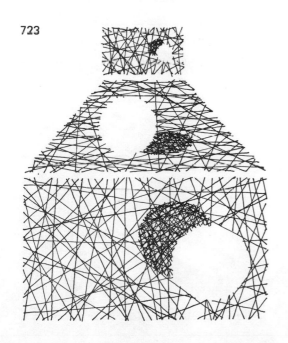

724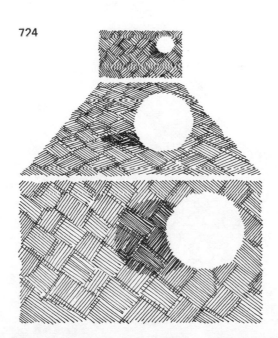

725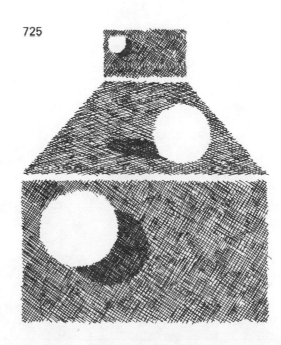

120

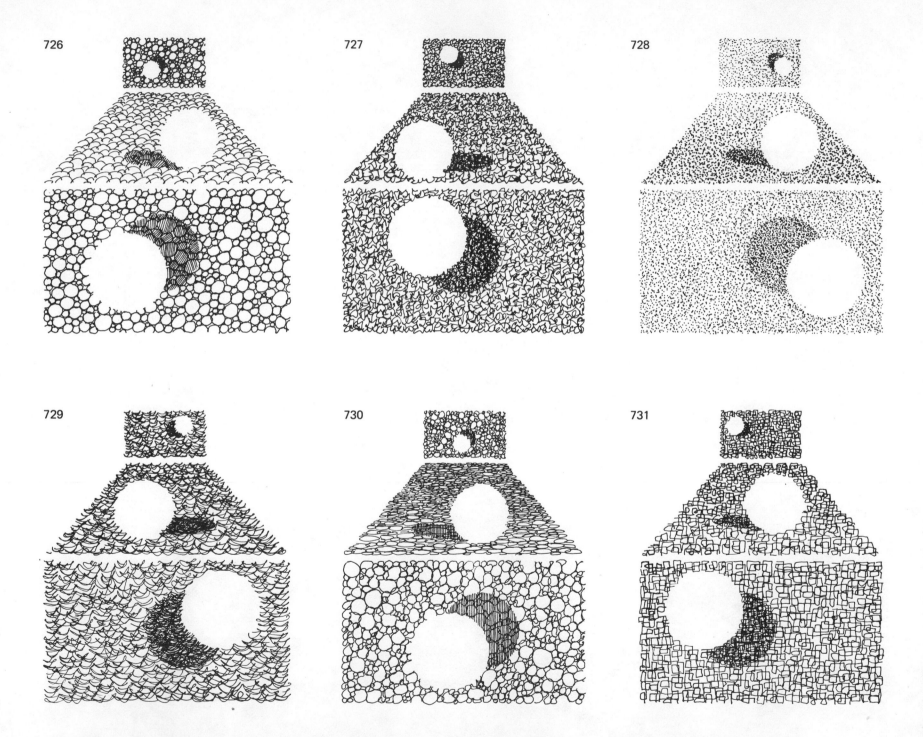

726   727   728

729   730   731

732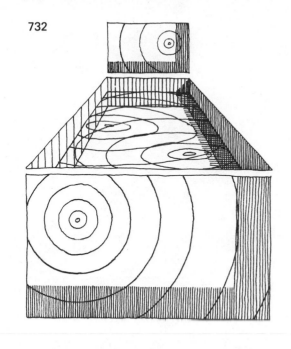

733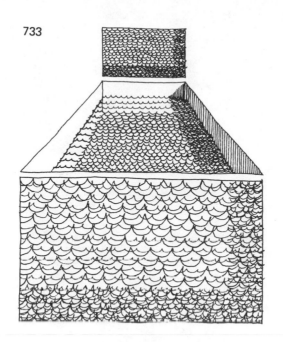

734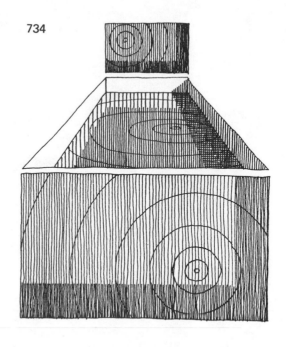

735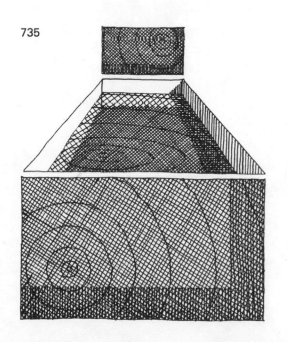

736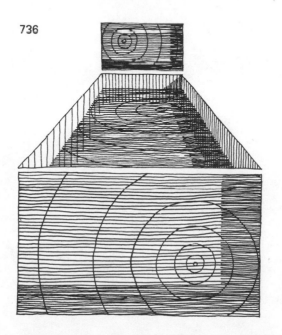

737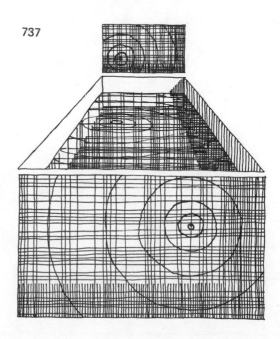

738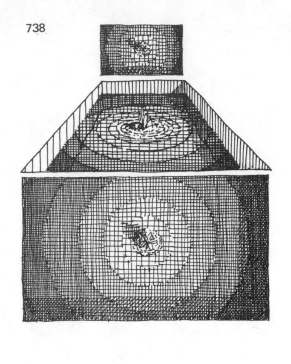

739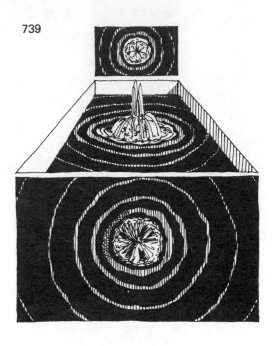

740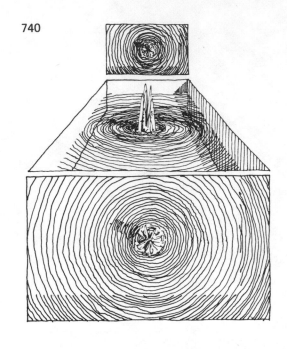

741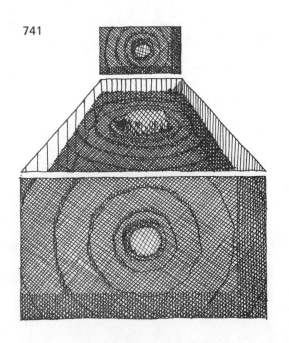

742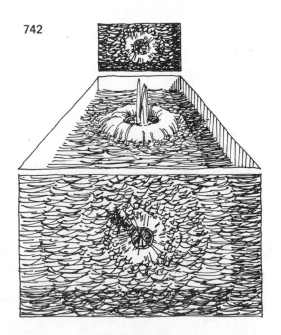

743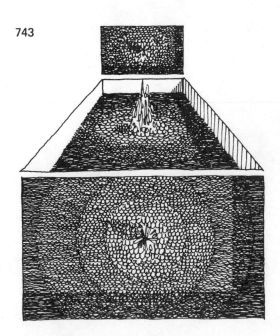

TREES IN PLAN

744

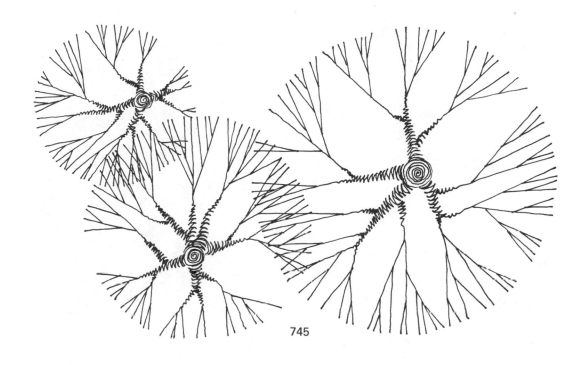

745

746

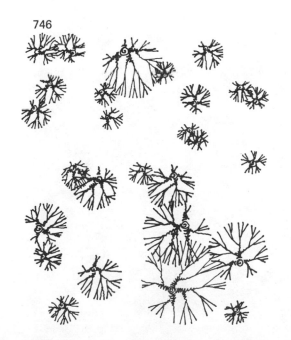

747

748

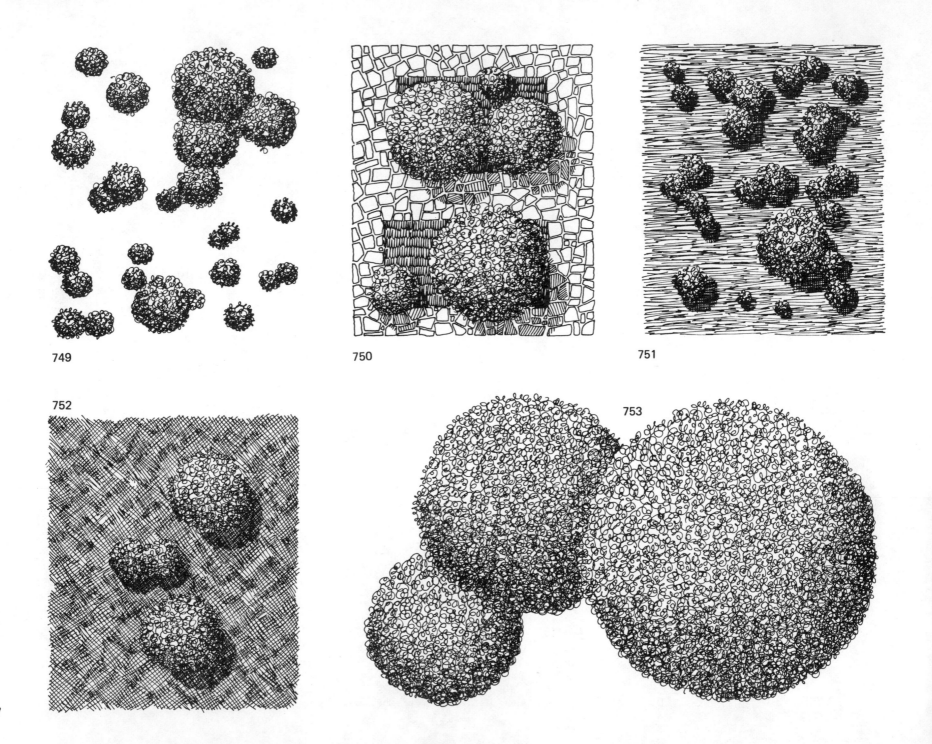

749

750

751

752

753

754

755

756

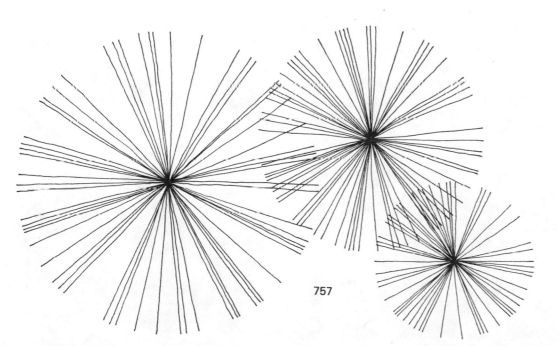

757

758

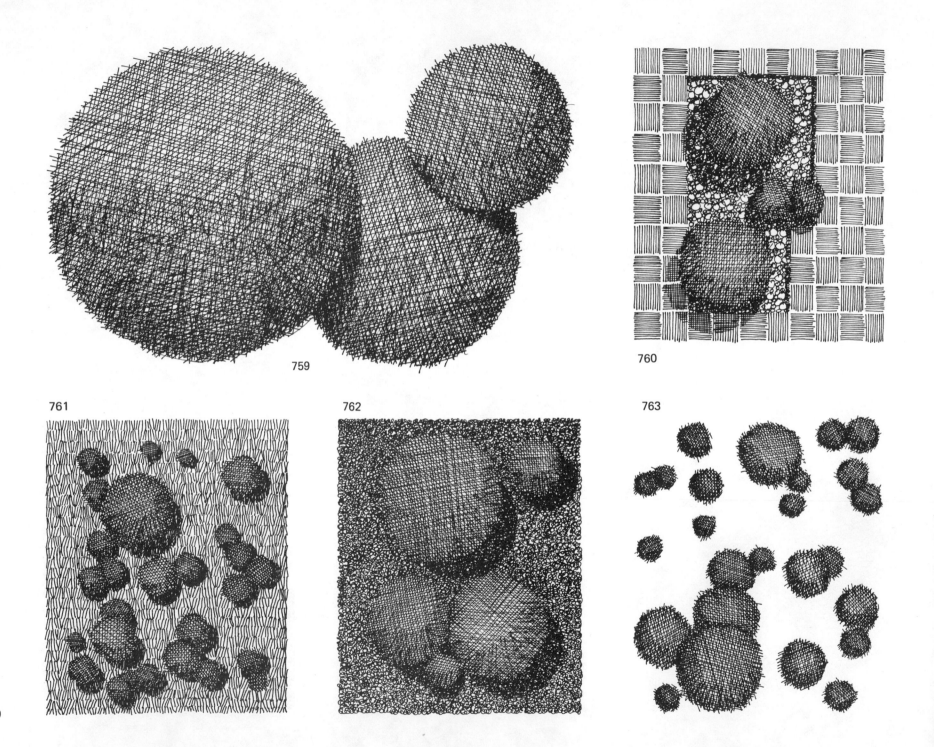

759

760

761

762

763

129

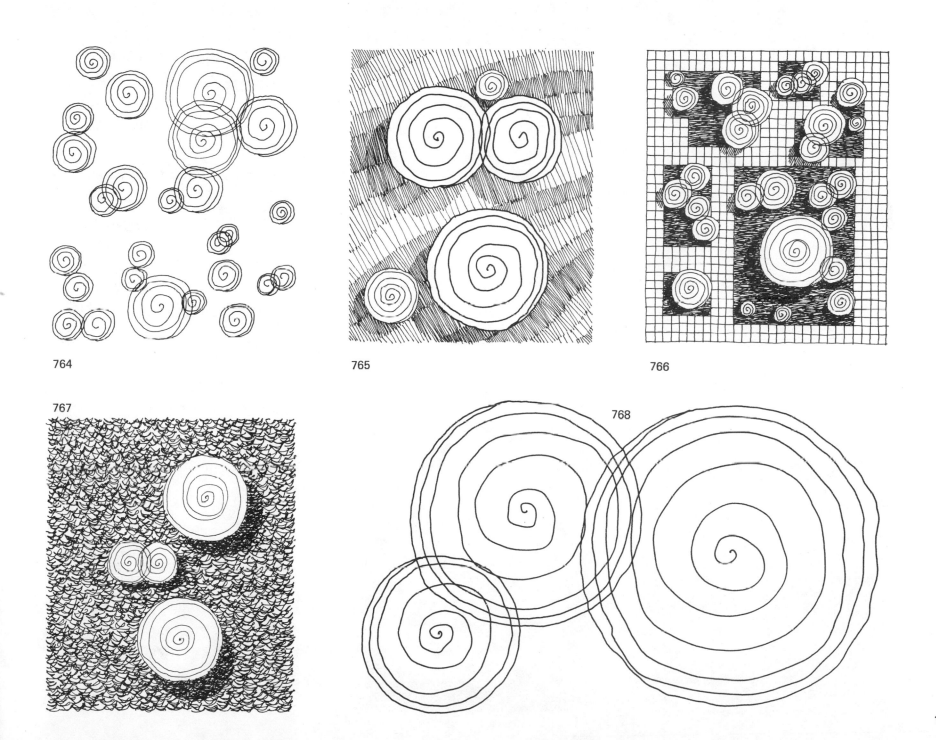

764

765

766

767

768

769

770

771

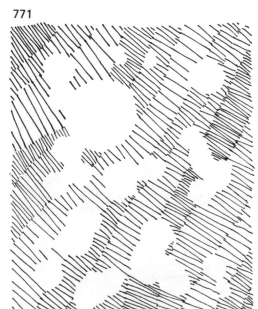

772

773

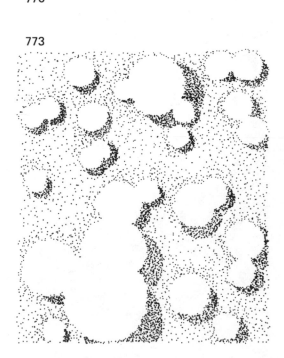

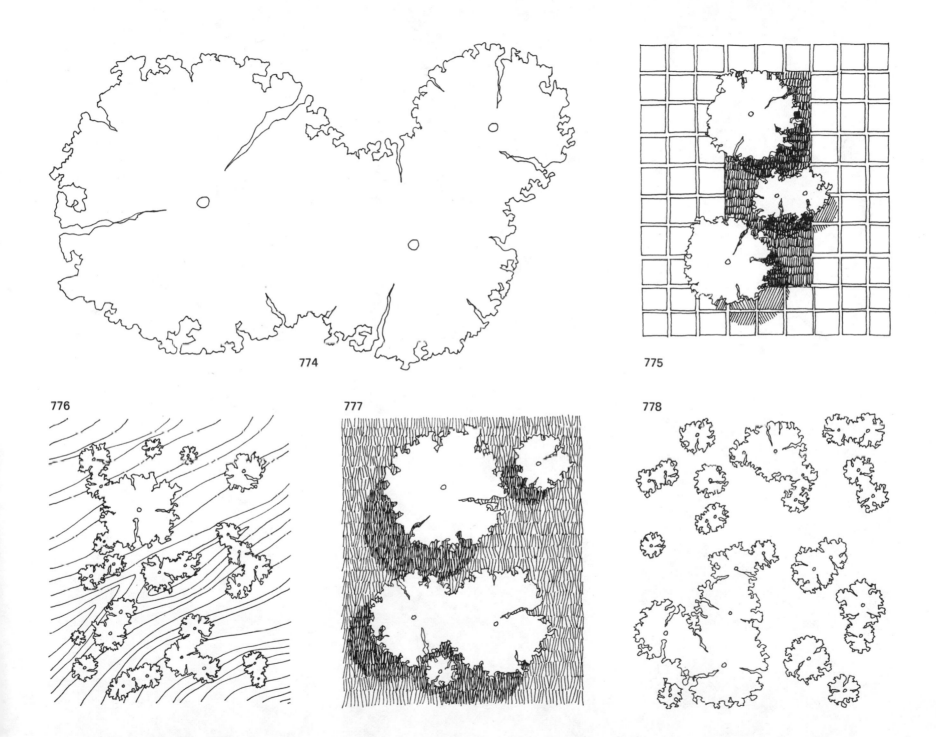

774

775

776

777

778

132

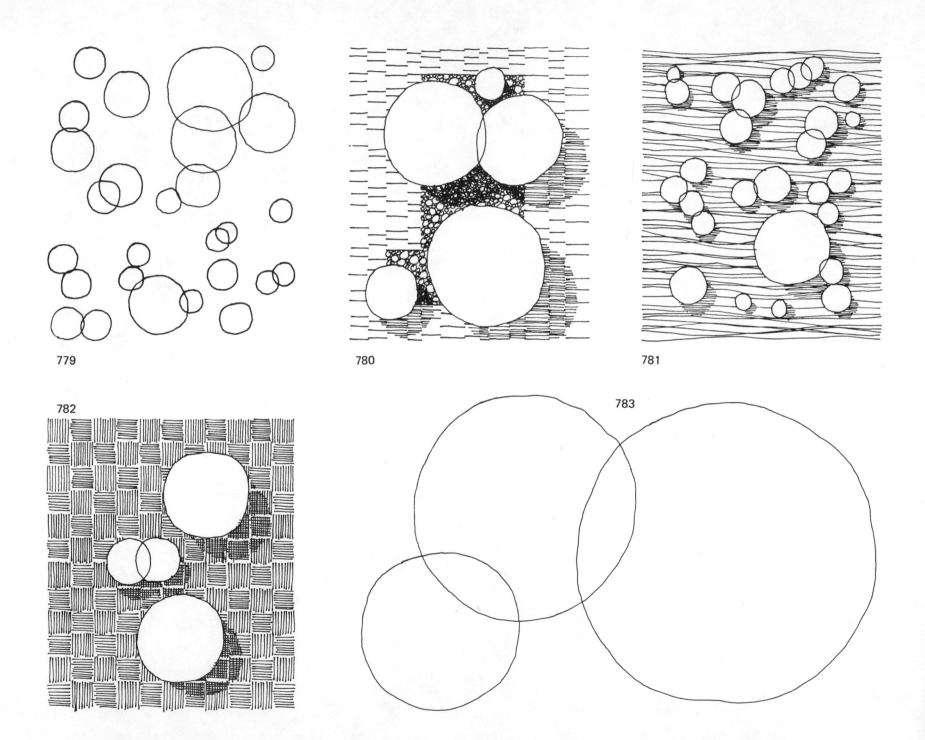

779

780

781

782   783

784

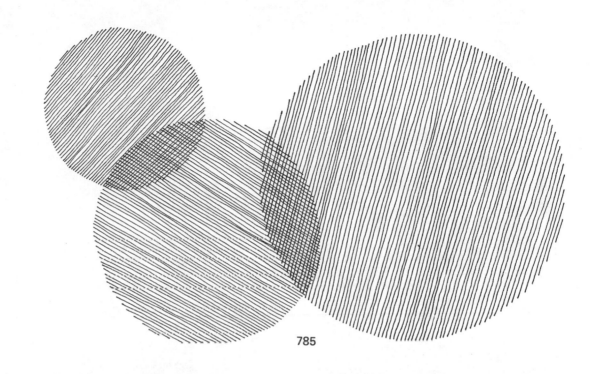

785

786

787

788

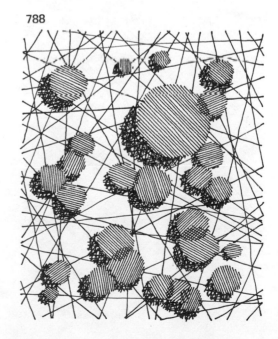

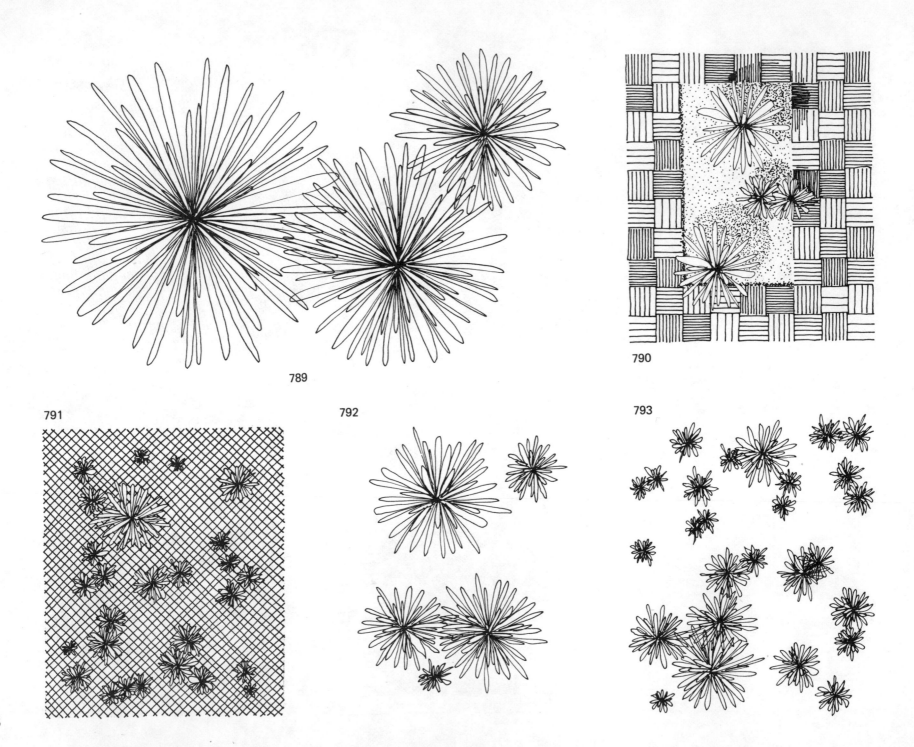

789

790

791

792

793

135

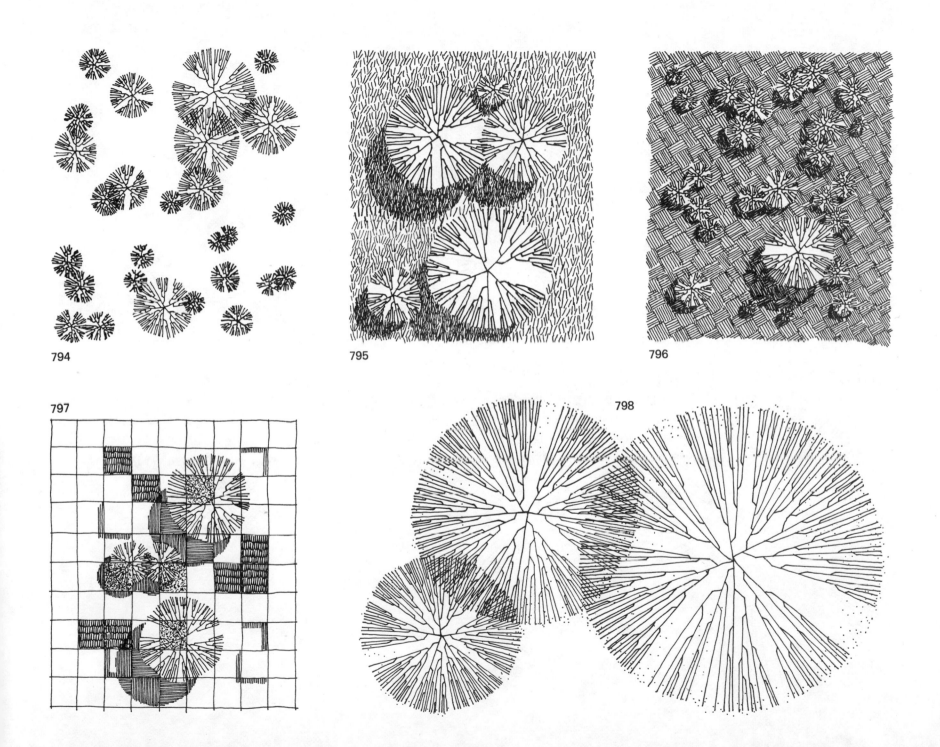

794

795

796

797

798

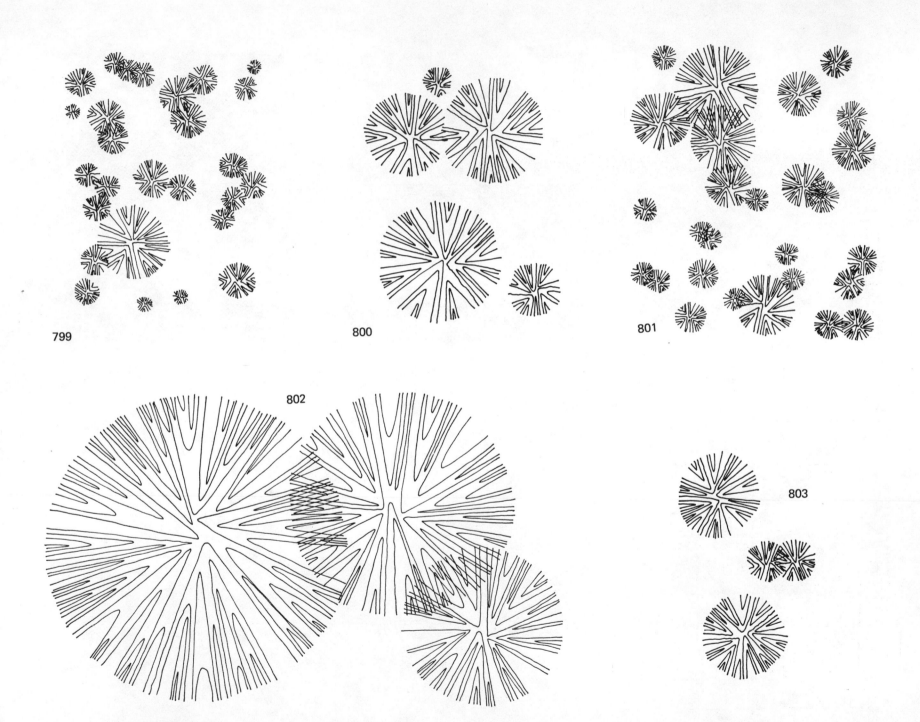

799

800

801

802

803

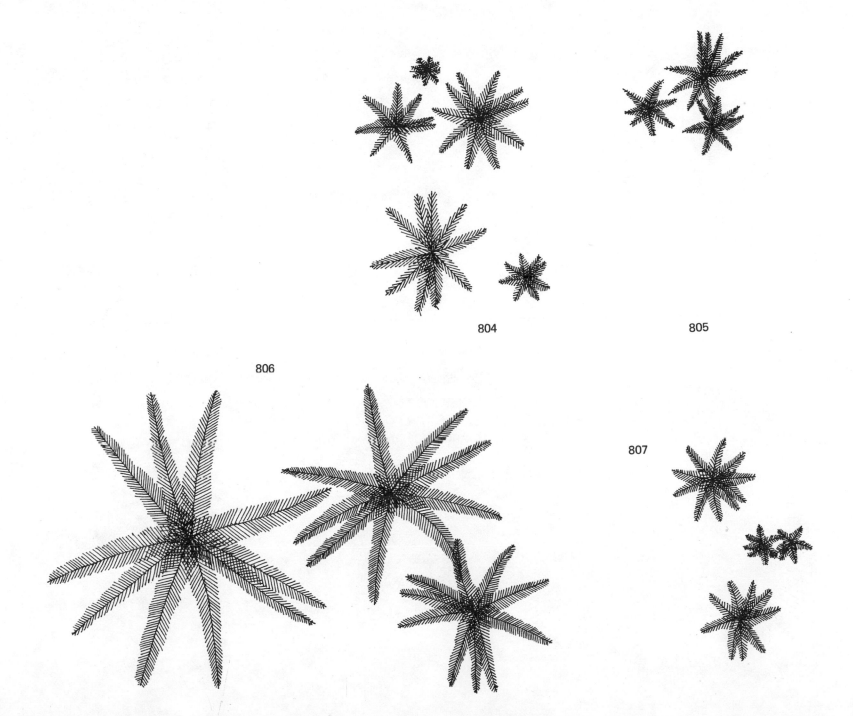

804

805

806

807

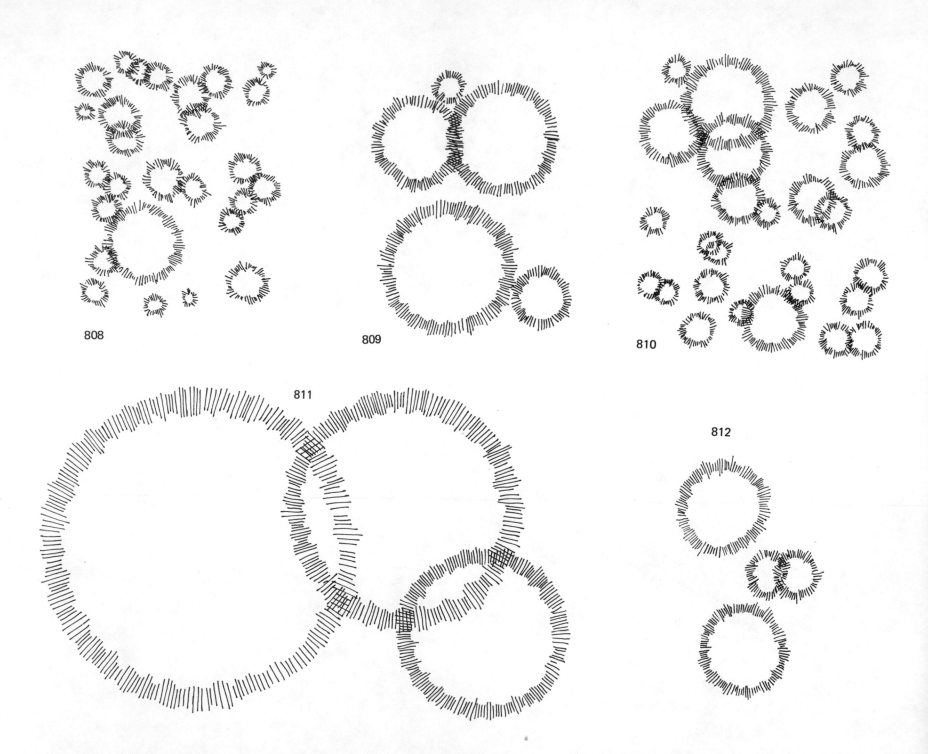

808

809

810

811

812

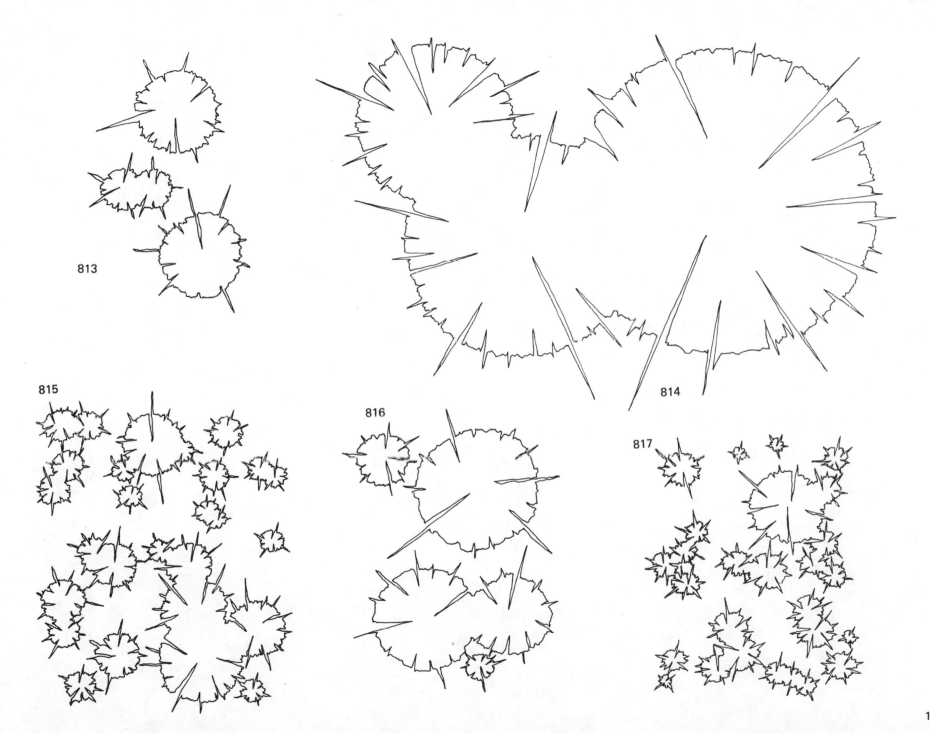

813

814

815

816

817

140

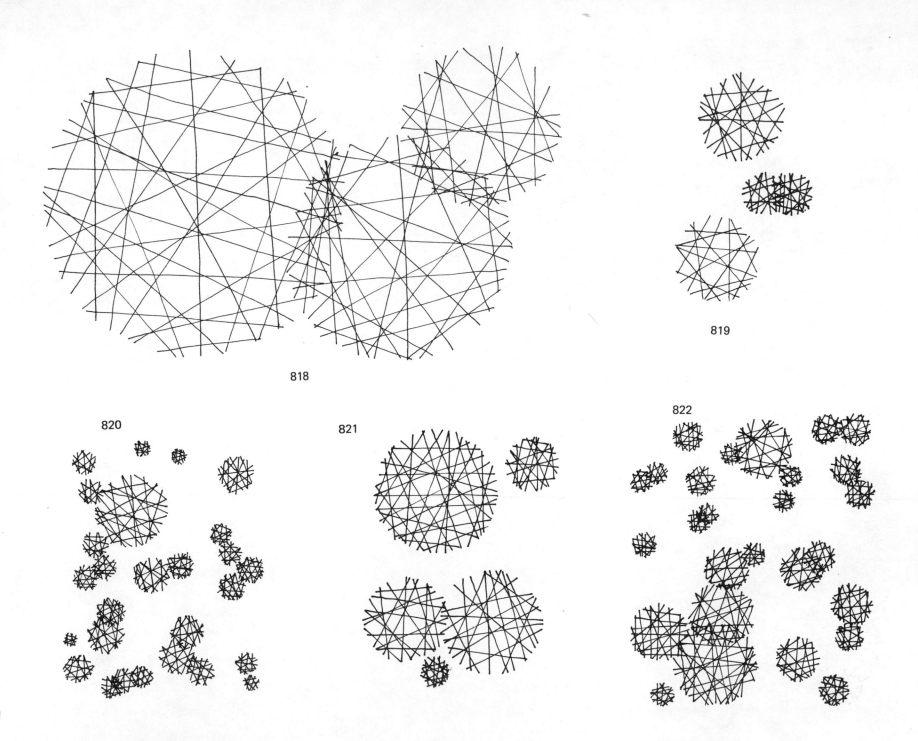

818

819

820

821

822

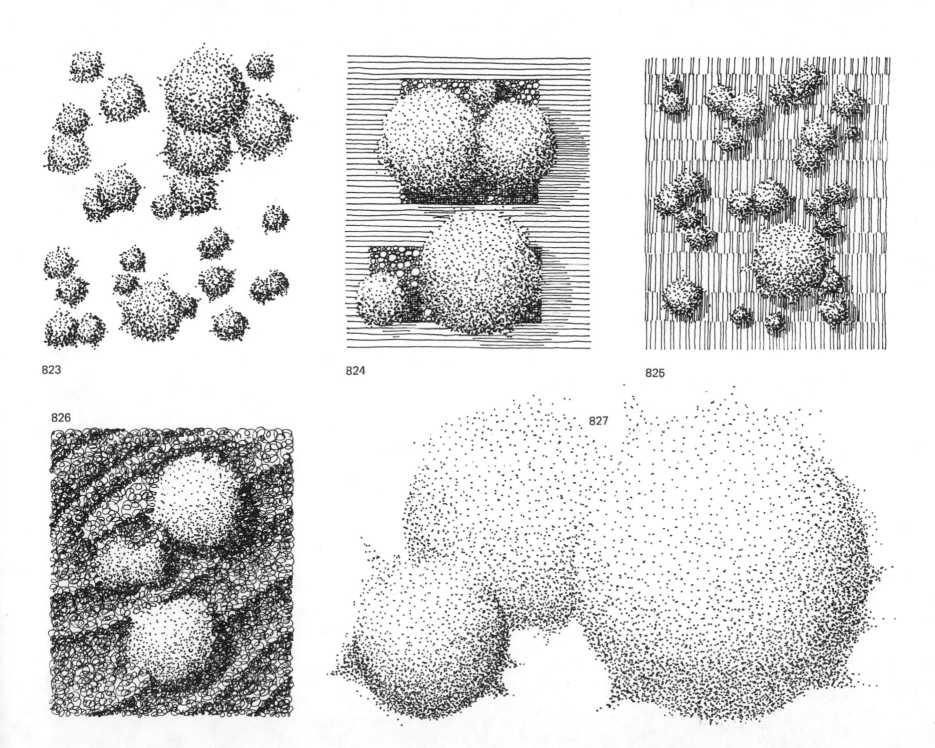

823

824

825

826   827

TREES IN ELEVATION

828

829

830

144

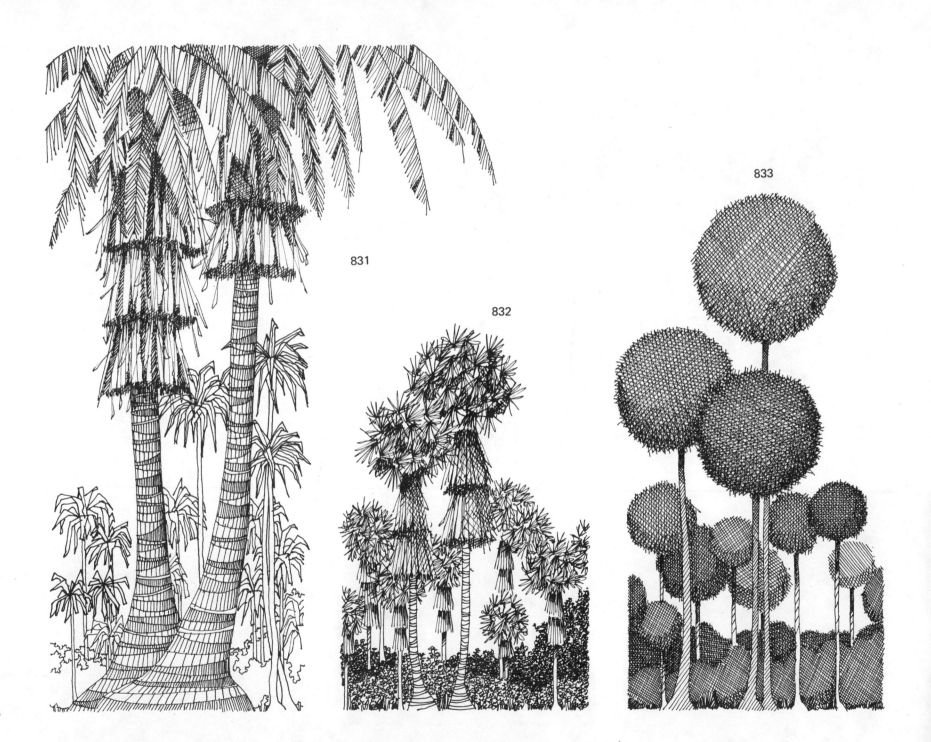

831

832

833

145

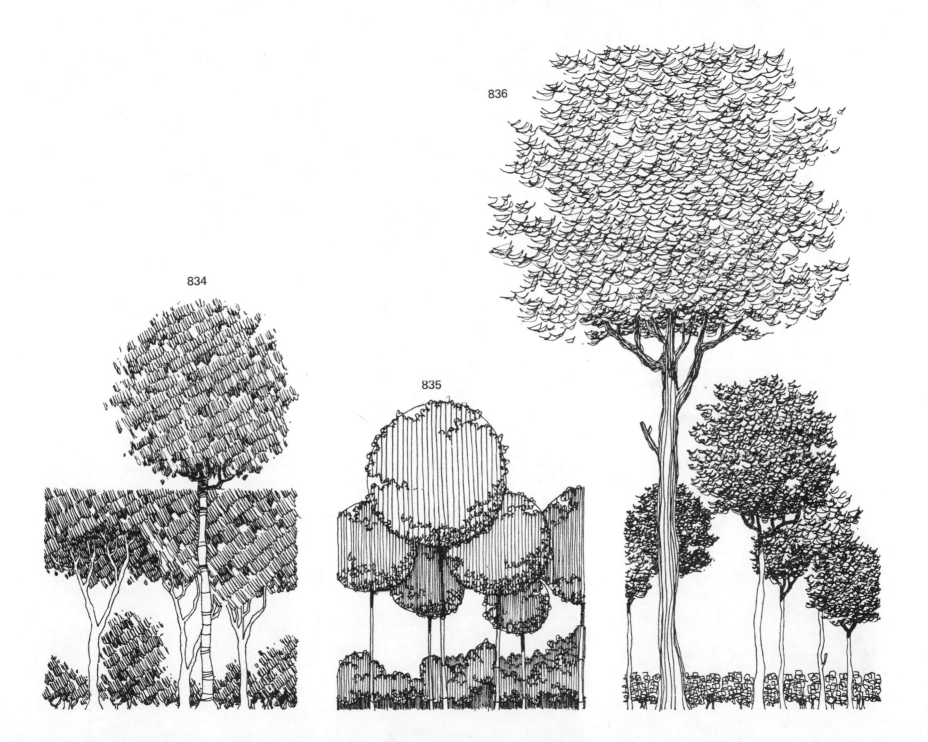

834

835

836

146

837

838

839

840

841

842

148

843

844

845

149

846

848

847

849

850

851

852

853

854

This chapter presents example vocabulary assemblies and illustrates some of the principles of relating the drawing components to each other. The drawings shown here are reduced to approximately half the original size. The book cover and chapter title pages are composed of sections of the drawings at full size. Samples of the traditional architectural presentation drawings are included. These are the site plan, plan, elevation, section, interior perspective and exterior perspective. Sectional perspective will be presented in a future edition. In using the graphic vocabulary there are some general principles which might be helpful in relating drawing components. Some of these apply more to some drawings than others. Placement of human figures, for example, deals more with perspective, section and elevation than with plan or site plan. The major vocabulary sections are listed below with some commentary on the use of each.

TEXTURES

The overall value scheme of a drawing should place visual emphasis on the building. • Adjacent material textures should have different values to insure distinct edges. • As plane directions change, the values of their surface materials should change. • Choose a sun direction which explains the building form best. • Try to complete textures against forms (rug against chair) to avoid white halos around forms. • Textures should be scaled to the scale of the drawing. • Know whether your drawing will be "windowed" (textures taken out to a rectangle) or vignetted (textures faded out at edges). Some textures are easier to fade out more successfully than others.

HUMAN FIGURES

Figures should be appropriate to the building type in terms of number, composition (male-female, adult-children), posture and dress. • Place the figures so that they are using the space (furniture, doors) and yet don't obscure critical architectural features (corners, details). • Relate the figures into appropriately sized groups. Try to avoid a room full of "loners". • Draw complete figures and relate them to the floor. Avoid cutting them off at the waist or legs. • Figures should be less detailed than the building. You are not selling clothes. • Use figures to set up a visual rythym leading to your building entry.

FURNITURE

Choose furniture appropriate to the building in terms of style and size. • Since furniture represents space use, choose views that explain furniture arrangement. • Draw complete furniture forms and relate them to the floor. Avoid cutting them off. • The building should be more detailed than the furniture. • Use accessories freely to show that the space is used (lighting, books, ash trays, plants, pots, paintings, sculpture.)

AUTOMOBILES

Place cars so that they don't obscure critical building elements. • Cars in the extreme foreground tend to be overdetailed because they are close to the viewer and because they take up so much of the drawing. • Relate all cars to the ground.

TREES

Tree indications in plan are generally interchangeable. They specify no particular type. • Trees should be drawn so as not to obscure or confuse plan elements. • Choose appropriate tree types in elevation for the building location. • Try to avoid station points that result in trees splitting the drawing in half or covering up important architectural details. • If possible, silhouette tree forms against the sky. Try to avoid drawing the building through the lacy texture of leaves and limbs.

SITE PLAN

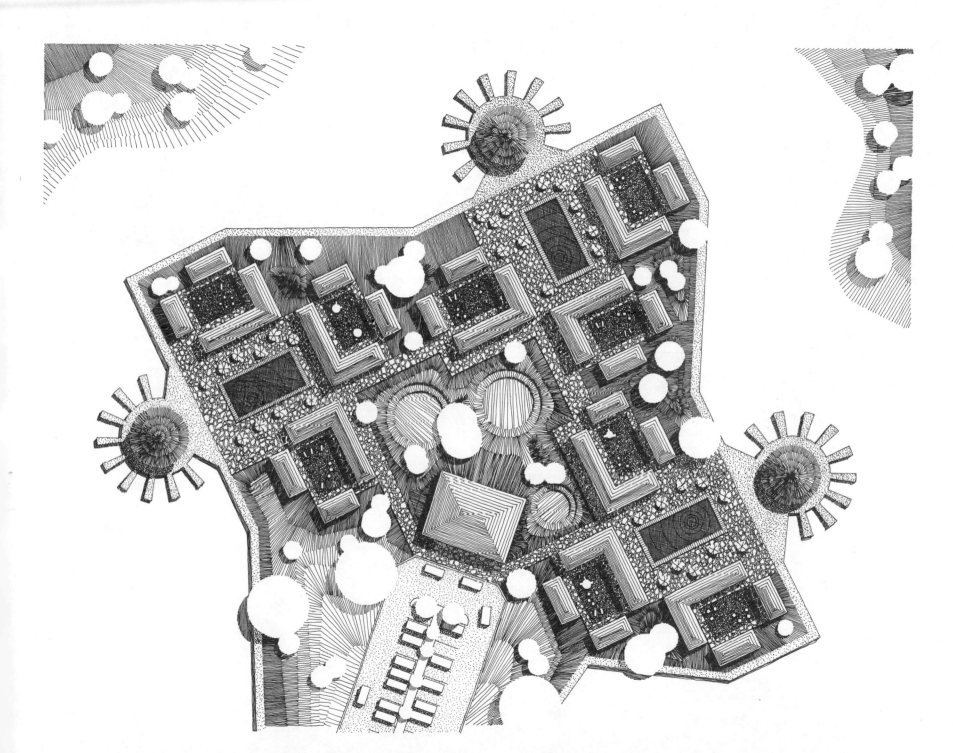

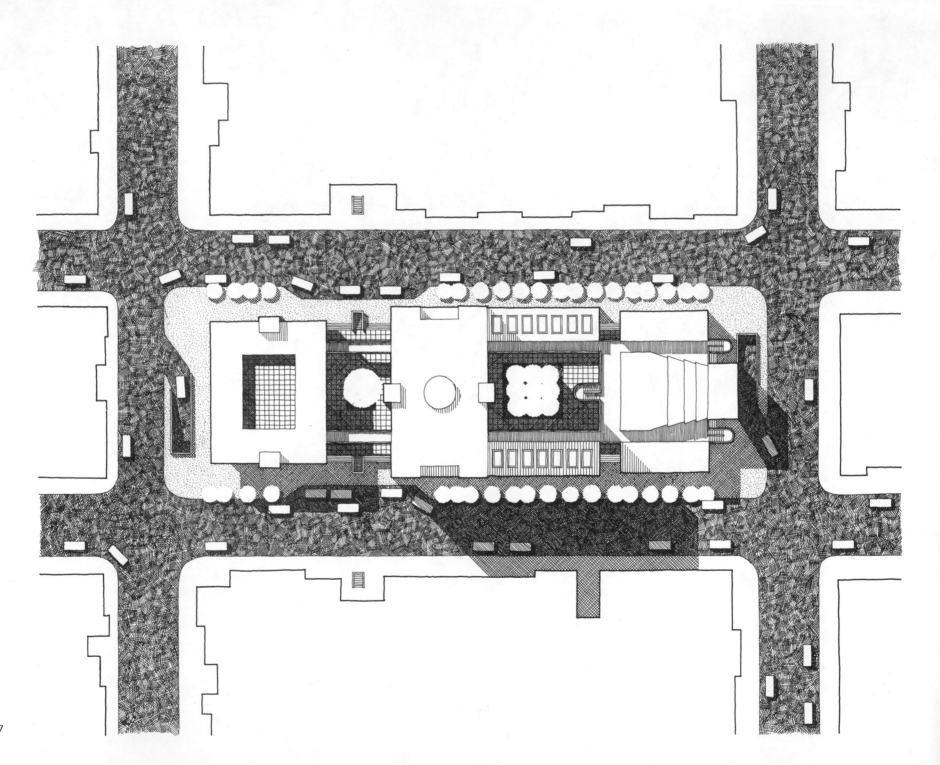

157

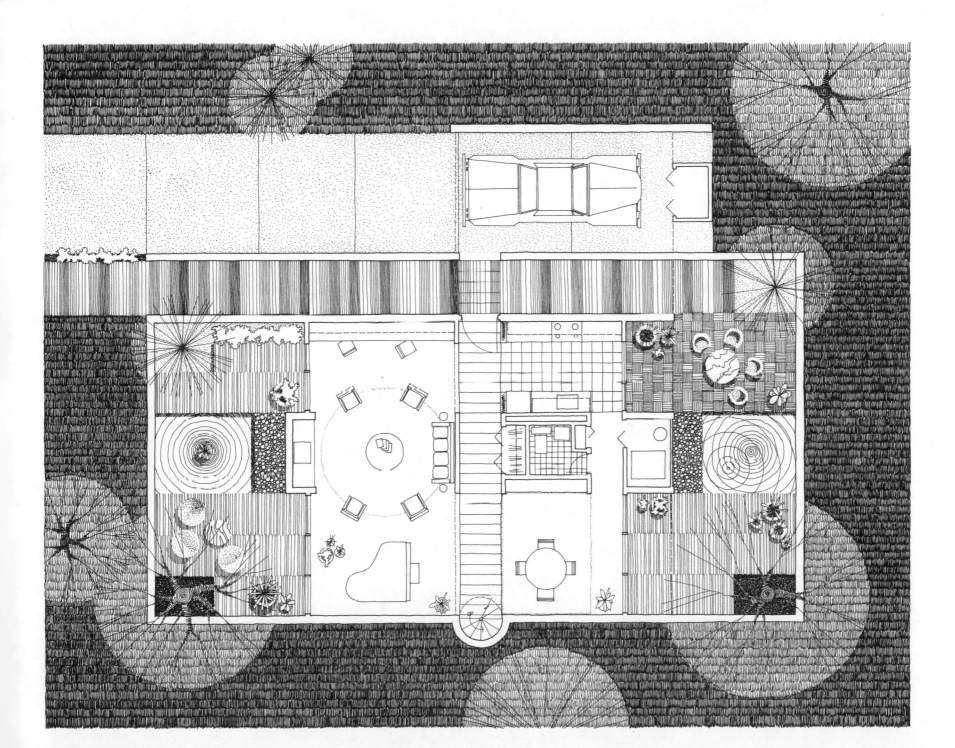

160

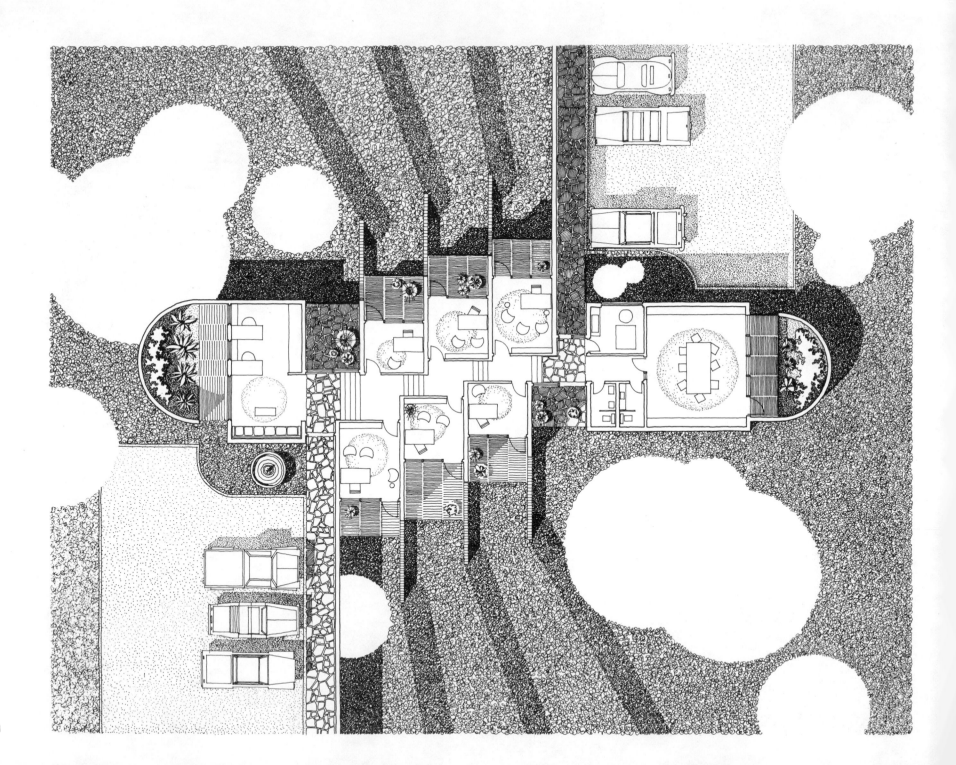

ELEVATION

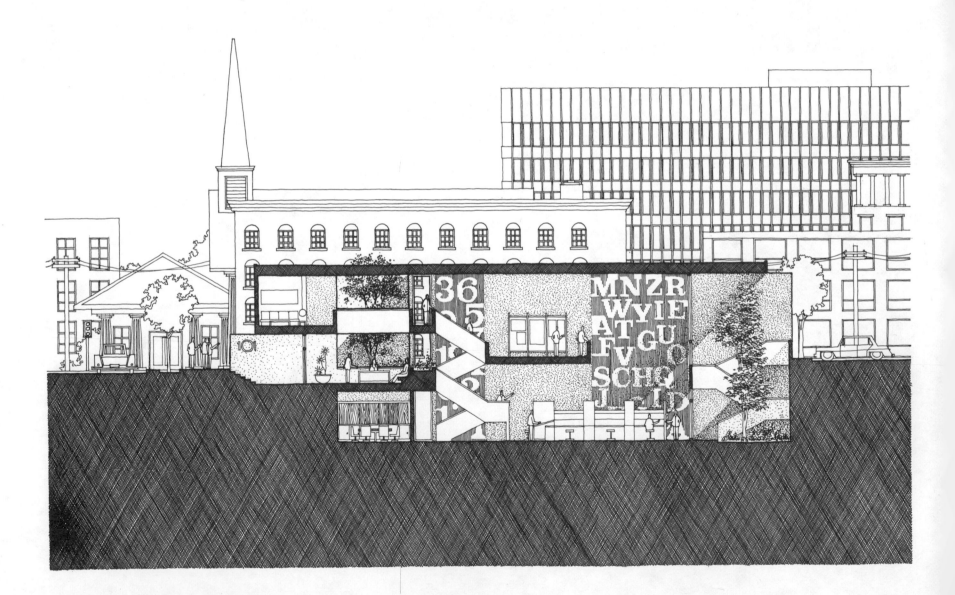

167

INTERIOR PERSPECTIVE

EXTERIOR PERSPECTIVE

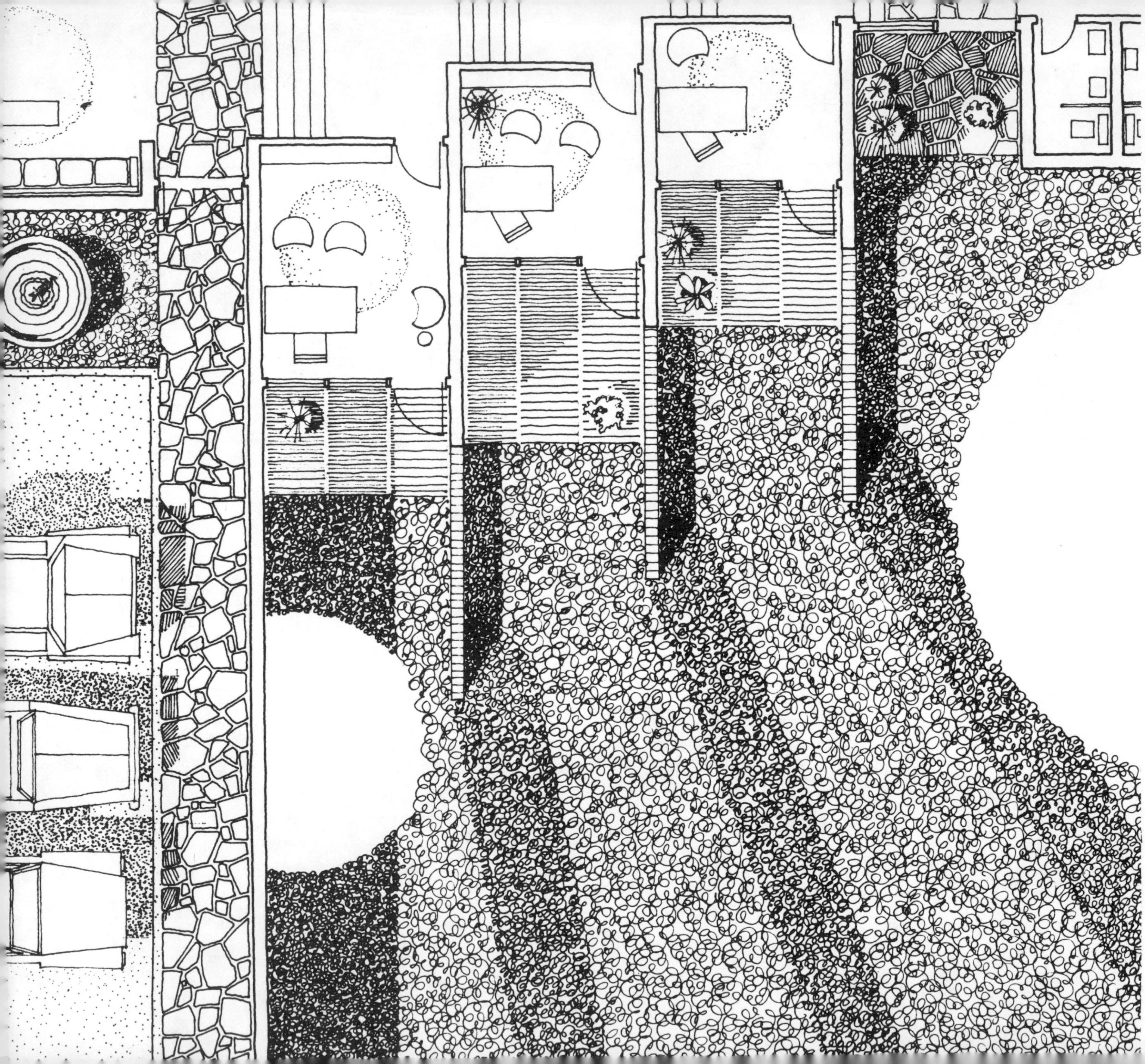

FIGURE LIST

PAGE	FIGURE	DESCRIPTION
73	396	CI Designs
73	397	CI Designs, Des. Warren Platner
73	398	CI Designs, Des. Bodil Kjaer
74	399	CI Designs, Des. Bodil Kjaer
74	400	CI Designs
74	401	CI Designs
75	402	CI Designs, Des. Hans Krieks
75	403	CI Designs, Des. Bill Bagnall
75	404	CI Designs, Des. Hans Krieks
75	405	CI Designs
76	406	CI Designs, Des. Bodil Kjaer
76	407	CI Designs
76	408	Scandiline, Des. A. Wahl-Iverson
76	409	Scandiline, Des. A. Fribyter, Borge Johnsson
77	410	Scandiline, Des. Inge Anderson
77	411	Stowe Davis
77	412	CI Designs, Des. Bodil Kjaer
77	413	CI Designs, Des. Warren Platner
78	414	CI Designs
78	415	Art Metal
78	416	CI Designs
78	417	CI Designs
79	418	Burke
79	419	Burke
79	420	Scandiline
80	421	CI Designs
80	422	Scandiline, Des. Sven Dyste
80	423	CI Designs, Des. Bodil Kjaer
81	424	Stowe Davis
81	425	Habitat, Des. Paul Mayen
81	426	Burke
81	427	CI Designs
82	428	Habitat
82	429	CI Designs, Des. Bodil Kjaer
82	430	CI Designs
83	431	Habitat, Des. Paul Mayen
83	432	CI Designs
83	433	Habitat
83	434	CI Designs, Des. Bodil Kjaer
83	435	Burke
83	436	Habitat, Des. Paul Mayen
84	437	Habitat
84	438	Burke
84	439	Habitat
84	440	Habitat
84	441	Habitat
84	442	Habitat
85	443	Habitat
85	444	Burke
85	445	Burke
85	446	CI Designs
86	447	Burke
86	448	Burke
86	449	Burke
86	450	Burke
86	451	Habitat
86	452	Burke
87	453	CI Designs, Des. Bodil Kjaer
87	454	Burke